T0209402

No Time to Waste

Microbehaviors: Leveraging the Little Things to Become a Better Leader

Artell Smith

iUniverse

NO TIME TO WASTE
MICROBEHAVIORS: LEVERAGING THE LITTLE
THINGS TO BECOME A BETTER LEADER

iUniverse books may be ordered through booksellers or by contacting:

iUniverse
1663 Liberty Drive
Bloomington, IN 47403
www.iuniverse.com
844-349-9409

ISBN: 978-1-6632-5120-6 (sc)
ISBN: 978-1-6632-4195-5 (hc)
ISBN: 978-1-6632-5121-3 (e)

Library of Congress Control Number: 2023903538

Print information available on the last page.

iUniverse rev. date: 03/24/2023

To Steve, Matt, Betsy, and Lisa

Legal Disclaimer

I'm not a lawyer and nothing in this work should be construed as legal advice. Each situation is unique, varying by people involved and the context of the interaction(s). If you need legal advice, you should contact your personal legal counsel, or in-house legal counsel, as appropriate. The stories and examples presented in this work arise from personal experiences. However, the names of individuals, locations, companies, details of the story, etc. have been adjusted to ensure anonymity of those described in the story. All hypothetical examples, as noted in the body of the text, carry names, facts, and circumstances to illustrate the content that is described and highlighted. Resemblance to any real person or authentic fact pattern is purely coincidental. Where needed, permissions have been obtained and granted to me to recount a story, or some of its elements.

CONTENTS

CONTENTS

FOREWORD

We're often told to see the big picture. We're pressured to skip molehills to concentrate on mountains. We're pushed to ignore the trees to see the forest. We're compelled to get out of the weeds and take a bird's-eye view. Countless sayings like these press us to look at issues as a whole.

But this push for a broader perspective has consequences. Wider views come at the cost of specifics. They urge us to skip the details and get to the point. This drive erodes focus. Our attention span shrivels, and we get overwhelmed.

What if there's a better way? What if mountains start as molehills? What if we can understand forests by seeing their trees? What if there's as much to learn in the weeds as in soaring with the eagles? Some of the most profound views come from taking a closer look. Perhaps tending to the small stuff better keeps it from ever becoming big stuff. Maybe the way to discover the most important picture is to look at the smaller picture.

Managers

Uplifting Impact is a diversity, equity, and inclusion (DEI) consultancy. Our approach explores how to create environments where everyone can thrive. We examine how fostering belonging helps organizations fulfill their objectives.

When team members become fuller versions of themselves, then organizations become fuller versions of themselves. Fundamental to this fulfillment are managers.

When executives support the DEI concept in the workplace, initiatives are successful 22 to 31 percent of the time. But when frontline leaders support them, even without C-suite backing, that number climbs to 42 to 46 percent. When direct supervisors uphold executive support, the total becomes greater than the sum of its parts. In fact, the success rate reaches 81 percent.[1]

Organizations can overhaul policies, procedures, and programs, but the success of those changes depends on managers. You can respond to all kinds of problems with top-level authority. But what causes change? Constant reminders and continuous reinforcement. In every meeting. During every huddle. At every check-in. The big picture only becomes real if it's upheld by managers.

What kind of work must managers do to achieve change? You guessed it: a lot of little things. People often tell us they want to focus on the *important* things. To create inclusivity, they want to overhaul their recruiting, hiring, and onboarding system. They're eager to spend big time, money, and energy revamping their mentoring; succession planning; and environmental, social, and governance impact reporting (ESG). But they dismiss how they interrupt their team members during meetings. They disregard the tone they use when emailing those who report to them. They don't care about scoffing at an employee during a brainstorming session. Why? They assume retention, problem-solving,

---

[1] Frances Brooks Taplett, Jennifer Garcia-Alonso, Matt Krentz, and Mai-Britt Poulsen, "It's Frontline Leaders Who Make or Break Progress on Diversity," BCG, March 5, 2020, www.bcg.com/publications/2020/frontline-leaders-make-break-progress-diversity.

accuracy, productivity, and profitability are the real indicators of organizational health. But there's something more.

Oftentimes, big things, such as salaries, board oversight, and market share, have less impact on organizational success than small things, such as encouraging participation, agreeing to suggestions, signaling interest, giving feedback, offering praise, and taking time to lighten the atmosphere. These simple things have profound results. They create a climate of functional communication. This qualitative environment leads to quantitative benefits. Managers who gain skills in these small things can see organizational success jump 59 percent regarding retention, problem-solving, accuracy, productivity, and profitability for two and a half years![2]

No Time to Waste

In *No Time to Waste*, Artell Smith discusses the key to unlocking this success: microbehaviors. You want to improve retention? Look to microbehaviors as a leadership solution. Want improved problem-solving? Practice the kind of microbehaviors that create positive vibes. Looking to foster the functional communication that creates organizational success? Implement the recognition, compliment, motivation, coaching, meeting, and communication strategies detailed throughout this book.

Smith notes that change is coming. Globalization, increasing diversity, and demographic shifts are changing the employee landscape. Even if you think you have no diversity where you are, drastic age reversals are on the way. The employee pool is flipping from majority baby boomers to

---

[2] Simone Kauffeld and Nale Lehmann-Willenbrock, "Meetings Matter: Effects of Team Meetings on Team and Organizational Success," *Small Group Research* 43, no. 2 (2012): 130–58.

majority millennials. That is the widest age shift ever. With it comes a seismic philosophical reversal.

Compared to previous generations, millennials spend more time at work. Because of this, their personal and professional worlds blend more than ever before. Older workers believed no news was good news, but people from underrepresented groups fear no news is proof they're on the verge of getting fired. As time passes, people from all populations want more from their work than punching a clock. They don't want to be worker robots. They want to work while retaining their humanity.

Managers are one of the primary forces that can rehumanize them. In a world where they are constantly taught to doubt their worth, what can help them regain the dignity essential to their reaching their full potential? *No Time to Waste* provides a brilliant answer. Your microbehaviors, compliments, smiles, and reinforcement are the keys to achieving big organizational success along the lines of recruitment, retention, and profitability. At the same time, they are vital to achieving something even more important: affirming people's full humanity.

Walking the Walk

Fundamental to recognizing the humanity of others is acknowledging our own. Important in that quest is to show vulnerability. By showing our teams that we are human, we allow them to be so. Few things achieve that more than modeling vulnerability. Ironclad leaders incite obedience, but enthusiasm is reserved for those with flesh and blood. Macrolevel toughness might be quicker, easier, and more familiar, but embracing microbehaviors is critical to unprecedented potential. When we share feelings, fears, and flaws in a productive way, we prove our humanity. Doing so is crucial to inviting others to be full humans.

This kind of brave leadership is core to Smith's approach. Modeling vulnerability, he invites others to do the same. Drawing from personal examples, even ones that are less than flattering, he allows readers to be colearners. Using stories from his life, Smith invites readers to see him as someone working, struggling, and succeeding alongside them in the quest to improve microbehaviors.

Next Steps

With specific tips, *No Time to Waste* makes it easy for readers to waste no time in putting these ideas into practice. These lessons on microbehaviors are structured for microlearning sessions. They contain opportunities for small discussions that bring these teachings to life so managers can start immediately building the interpersonal relationships that lead to long-term organizational success.

On a personal level, Smith's work has been key to broadening our approach to DEI work. *No Time to Waste* has us thinking about the microbehaviors that lead to programmatic changes, and we're humbled and grateful that the book has added this nuance to our thinking. Given how it's evolved our own perspective, we're confident it will do the same for you. To make big changes, all we must do is follow the advice outlined in *No Time to Waste* and make room to practice thinking small picture.

—Deanna Singh
Managing partner, Uplifting Impact, and author of
Actions Speak Louder: A Step-by-Step Guide to Becoming

an Inclusive Workplace and *Purposeful Hustle: Direct Your Life's Work Towards Making a Positive Impact*
—Justin Ponder, PhD
Chief information officer, Uplifting Impact, and professor at Marian University of Fond du Lac

PREFACE

Big Things versus Small Things

Successful business leaders are always looking for ways to improve how we manage our companies or organizations. If we're proactive, we read leadership books, attend workshops and seminars, and actively participate in coaching and mentorship programs designed to help business leaders do their jobs more effectively. Many of us have long been taught not to sweat the small stuff but, rather, to focus solely on the big-picture issues that are likely to impact the company in a positive or negative way. While it may sound counterintuitive, we have been looking at things upside down. We really should sweat the small stuff, and at the core is the concept of microbehaviors in the workplace.

What is a microbehavior? A microbehavior is a short phrase or brief action, or series of them, that conveys meaning quickly and efficiently. The impact is generally immediate—and always positive when done right. When a microbehavior is not done right, however, the impact is always negative and hard to recover from. That's why it's so important to understand the important role our words, facial expressions, tone of voice, and body language play in every interaction we have at work.

For example, starting a conversation by saying you're glad to see the person instead of immediately jumping right into the issue at hand is a microbehavior you can consciously manage. So is standing when a client or new employee enters a room, as well as greeting the person with an appropriate handshake. It may seem minor, but showing respect for the individual by standing up to shake his or her hand before the start of the meeting will set the tone for the conversation that follows. The simple act of texting a quick note of thanks to an employee who did well on a given day is a microbehavior that takes less than one minute but will have a lasting positive impact on the employee who receives the text.

Over nearly forty years in the business world, I've had the good fortune of knowing many fine leaders and managers. From my first experiences in a corporate setting, I've been coached and developed by some of the best. My longtime mentor Steve King—author of *Six Conversations* and *Brag, Worry, Wonder, Bet*—has exhibited great patience in helping me through a variety of challenging situations. I'm indebted to him in almost every way. But he's not the only mentor I've had. Others have come along, and some have moved on. When I refer to a mentor throughout this book, I'm talking about several different people. I include conversations with my mentor, like the one that follows, in various chapters to illustrate core concepts and ideas. They're basically drawn from a composite of my many mentors I've had over the decades in the corporate arena.

In some cases, coaching from my mentor involved big things with the potential for large, impactful change. In other cases, my mentor's coaching involved small things with the potential for small but also impactful change. I learned over time that my mentor was sincere about both small things and big things. He was big into learning about how to manage my microbehaviors as a business leader. In short, he emphasized the little things much more than he focused on big-picture issues.

Below is an example of what I'm talking about, in terms of both mentor dialogue and microbehaviors that can produce positive results in the workplace.

My Mentor and Me

MENTOR. I heard you're going to talk to Mary about her performance.

ARTELL. Yes, it's going to be difficult. Not really looking forward to it. She will probably be surprised.

MENTOR. What will you say first?

ARTELL. I'll talk about how the project is failing and her role in that.

MENTOR. No, I mean what are the words you will use to start the conversation?

ARTELL. Um, I don't know. Something like "Things have not been going well with the project, and I want to talk to you about it now."

MENTOR. I have a suggestion. Start out by asking Mary these questions: "How do you think the project is going? What concerns do you have?"

ARTELL. OK. I think jumping in is fine, but I'll ask your questions first.

Was the above conversation a small thing? Definitely. It involved coaching for one specific conversation, with one suggested opening. It took no more than a minute during a stop-in visit to my mentor's office. Was the suggested approach impactful? Yes, especially for Mary, to whom I was giving feedback. Rather than putting Mary on the defensive, the questions suggested by my mentor got Mary talking more freely without feeling that I was there to administer punishment of some kind. I also learned several things in the conversation with Mary that altered my viewpoint on how to coach her going forward. It was a win-win situation.

I also recall clearly a big-thing conversation with my mentor. My mentor was the chief learning officer of the company. I was the learning leader for a large and growing business area.

My Mentor and Me

MENTOR. The other HR leaders are worried about the manager development work you're doing. They feel that you haven't been communicating with them.

ARTELL. Why should they be worried? It doesn't really affect them. My business-area leadership have agreed to the work, and we're moving forward.

MENTOR. HR leaders across the enterprise are your colleagues. Their expectations are reasonable. Manager development work can impact them too.

ARTELL. Are you saying I need to get their buy-in and permission before I move forward? My business-area leadership haven't said anything about the need for me to do so.

MENTOR. No, I'm worried you're getting ahead of yourself by not keeping them informed. The success of your business area is their concern too. And business leaders across the company talk all the time, with the development of managers of high interest to them. What benefits can you see if you give them a chance to ask questions and make suggestions?

ARTELL. I get it. Makes sense. Let me put something together for them.

Was this conversation a big thing? You bet. My mentor's advice and suggestions opened my eyes to what was needed to make our manager development efforts really rock 'n' roll. All told, it took about one hour. The conversation was on point, and like most pointy conversations, it stung a bit. But I immediately went back to my desk and drafted a lengthy note to my fellow HR leaders across the company, explaining the manager development work I was spearheading. The result? Helpful suggestions, improved trust, clear support, and, ultimately, a successful, high-impact program for managers.

Big things, which require more time, effort, concentration, and preparation, are essential to being a good leader or manager. My mentor planned what he was going to say to me; picked the right location—out of view of almost everyone; and executed the conversation perfectly. The impact changed my behaviors over a long period of time. In my case, the behavioral impact has lasted more than twenty-five years! A success.

Small things, which require less time, effort, and preparation, are also essential to being a good leader or manager. Frequently, small things occur spontaneously, in situations where you need to react quickly and clearly. Once upon a time, I attended a class called Small Things Count, which was about client etiquette, including which fork or spoon to use at a fancy dinner. Using the large fork or the small fork isn't the focus of this book, however, probably to your great relief! But this book is about short encounters you have in which you can make an immediate impact, using short phrases that convey your meaning quickly and efficiently. Am I talking about coaching interactions? Yes, but not exclusively and not in the classic sense of the term, which usually implies a process. I'm suggesting instead that coaching be viewed narrowly through short interactions.

Small-thing interactions can be about a person, a place, a situation, a context, a culture, or a project or program. Small-thing interactions can improve a situation greatly, or they can make it much worse. Throughout the book, the language I'll be using to refer to small things will be characterized by the word *micro*. A small-thing interaction is a microinteraction. Microinteractions consist of microbehaviors. I'll attach the word *micro* to many different concepts—for example, microinclusion, microrecognition, microreward, microinfluence, microcoaching, microquestioning, and others.

However, I won't attach *micro* to the word *management*. Micromanagement isn't the subject of this book. The opposite of *micro*, *macro*, is also not the focus of this book. I won't be delving into macrobehaviors other than to say a series of microbehaviors can lead to amazing, powerful macro-outcomes.

Chapters of this book don't necessarily build on one another. Each chapter should stand on its own and can be used for microlearning moments. Most chapters deal with either one microbehavior or a related set of microbehaviors.

Lastly, the stories I relate throughout the book are all true. However, I've changed the names and, in some cases, the location or company where the interaction happened. I've used the names of friends and relatives throughout the book too. Unless specifically stated, the people in the story do not go by the names I have assigned. Please see the Legal Disclaimer at the front of the book for more information.

Let's dive into the concept of microbehaviors and how you can consciously make an effort to identify and manage them. The payoff will be almost immediate in improved employee morale, productivity, and retention. A happier workplace is a side benefit of immense value. You're in the driver's seat. Now hit the gas and begin your journey to becoming an even more effective business leader.

1

Understanding Microbehaviors

In the preface, I defined a microbehavior as a small, short, detectable action or phrase. The key to better managing your own microbehaviors is to first be aware of what they are, both in a positive and in a negative manner.

Here are some possible positive microbehaviors:

- Starting a conversation with "So glad to see you today! I don't want to tackle this tough issue without you."
- Standing up when a client or new employee enters a room and greeting her with a handshake and a smile.
- Bringing in everyone's favorite bagels for all to enjoy, with no fanfare.
- Including, in a project email, a congratulatory comment about a team member who went above and beyond.
- Texting a team member "You made a big impact today, and I hope you know how much we appreciate you."

I've coached employees and managers over the years to use microbehaviors to maintain or expand the self-esteem of others. The connection to improved engagement should be obvious as well. In the long run, constant and consistent use of positive microbehaviors can make work life more enjoyable and productive. Your employees are more likely to engage in transparent, candid discussions with you and recognize that you're their supporter, not a detractor.

Negative Microbehaviors

Unfortunately, you also can have the reverse situation with microbehaviors, which can sometimes come across as negative. I'd like to think that as I've matured, I've been able to eradicate negative microbehaviors. Sadly, that is not always the case. A short negative comment, discussion, or interaction can be enormously damaging and tough to overcome. Have you ever been in a discussion where you said something and immediately thought, *Oh Lord, I wish I hadn't said that*? Bingo. That's a negative microbehavior. Some examples include the following:

- Starting a conversation with "About time. You're late, but not to worry; the problem is almost solved."
- Greeting a new employee with "Oh, today is your first day? Gosh, totally slipped my mind. Bad day for me. Let's talk soon."
- Bringing your favorite doughnuts into the office and saying, "Hey, guys, come and get it. Best doughnuts on the planet. I'll eat them if you don't!"
- Including this comment in a project email: "Please don't Reply All on this email. Enough wrong things have been done already."

- Texting a team member, "We're still here working, and maybe you should shelve your plans and come back."

I remember one painful example of a microbehavior that has stuck with me. I supported a business leader who could exhibit significant impatience from time to time. Occasionally, the impatience was directed toward me. I once sent an email to the leader with an impassioned plea about a program, and the leader responded with "k." Just the one lowercase letter. Nothing else.

The "k" was a microbehavior within the meaning of our definition, and it carried a huge amount of weight when I read it. What did that one lonely letter mean? Knowing the leader, it meant, "Go ahead with what you want, but I think I wouldn't handle it this way." The leader didn't provide an explanation and left me to make up a story. This negative microbehavior drained my confidence. Just one letter! In checking with others, I was relieved to find out that I wasn't the only one who had received a "k" in response to a complex email. That made me feel a little better.

Conversely, this same leader was capable of microbehaviors that had the exact opposite effect on me. In response to a report about an employee-relations situation that had ended well, the leader responded with "great" in an email. The response was all lowercase, but the message was clear to me, and I took it to heart: "I'm glad you were able to work this out. The employee is in a better spot, and the company benefits too."

Strictly speaking, I probably read too much into both the "k" email and the "great" email. But in the latter case, it was a smorgasbord of positive intent containing five whole letters! We take what we can get when it comes to recognition, right? "Great" was recognition to me, and I made of it what I could. This microbehavior could also be considered a microrecognition, just as the "k" was a microbehavior that was, in fact, a microcritique.

I've become fond of the term *microcritique* to indicate a moment of feedback, with a supposed developmental flavor, that's intended to show displeasure. A microcritique is not a microaggression, as I'll talk about in chapter 5. We all know how it feels to be the victim of a microcritique, a casual slight stated in a matter-of-fact way. Such a critique could almost be missed if not for the emotion that it engenders in the receiver, thus my feelings about the "k" I received from the leader in the story above.

Behavioral Precalibration

We've all been in situations where we innocently said the wrong thing and probably also some situations where we were intentional in what we said and not so innocent. How do we restructure cognitively to allow for a new, better behavior to manifest versus an old, bad behavior? There's an intriguing concept in psychology called cognitive restructuring. I'm not an expert, but the process is one that helps people to divest themselves of negative thinking patterns, called cognitive distortions.

Unfortunately, there are many possible cognitive distortions that someone could fall prey to. Cognitive restructuring is a concept adjacent to microbehaviors and the management of them, though at its root, cognitive restructuring is designed to help resolve challenging mental illnesses. Albert Ellis in the 1950s and Aaron T. Beck in the 1960s were basically the dual ground zeros for cognitive restructuring. Reading about their research and its applications got me thinking.

I'm pretty good at coaching leaders and managers when it comes to exhibiting productive behaviors in organizational settings. Conceptually, a tiny bit of knowledge about cognitive restructuring sent me down a road. To start, let's use a different label to center ourselves: *behavioral precalibration*. It trips right off the tongue, doesn't it? Using the word *behavioral* is obvious, but why *precalibration*? Because we should try to think through the microbehavior before the rest of the world can see and experience it.

I believe we can conceptualize the microbehavior in a microinstant of time. How fast can we think? Really fast! We can take in approximately eleven million bits of data and information at one time. We can pay attention to about forty. Among the forty things we're paying attention to, we can grab on to a few, in a microinstant, to behaviorally precalibrate. Microbehavioral intentionality. As my grandmother said, "Think before you speak." It's sound advice upon which I reflect frequently.

Putting things together, behavioral precalibration is the technique that'll help you more clearly see the "What's in it for me?" aspect of thinking before you speak. Spending a microinstant to precalibrate will allow for just enough judgment to be applied before the microbehavior escapes into the environment. The benefit is clear since correcting for an old, bad behavior is a lot more work than enjoying the new, good behavior and its impact. How many times will you need to behaviorally precalibrate until the new, good behavior is routine? As many times as it takes until you get it right!

Below, on the left are examples of unprecalibrated, negative comments, and on the right are precalibrated, positive comments.

Negative Microbehaviors	Positive Microbehaviors
• Saying to the leader of the meeting, "Seems like we never make it through your agenda in our meetings."	• Saying to the leader of a meeting, "Your work to prep for our meetings makes a positive difference in achieving goals."
• Saying to an employee, "I want to hear more about that," but always canceling the meeting.	• Saying to an employee, "I want to hear more about that," and scheduling time to do so.
• Saying, "Merry Christmas," to a Muslim employee.	• Saying, "Merry Christmas," to a Christian employee.
• Saying to an employee who has never mentioned football, "I can't wait for the Super Bowl!"	• Saying to an employee who is a sports fan, "I can't wait for the Super Bowl!"
• Saying to an employee in a wheelchair, "Seems like it would be a lot easier for you to work from home."	• Saying to an employee in a wheelchair, "How can we make the afternoon meeting easier and more accessible for you?"
• Saying to a heavy-set employee, "You know, I have great ideas for you to lose those extra pounds."	• Saying to a heavy-set employee nothing about his or her weight.

The Precalibration Process

Let's imagine you're meeting for the first time a young nonbinary person. *Nonbinary* refers to someone whose gender is neither male nor female. Other terms could also apply, such as *genderqueer, agender,* or *bigender.*[3] Some nonbinary persons prefer to be addressed as *they* or *them,* while others prefer *he* and *him* or *she* and *her.* There is no one answer on how to address someone who is nonbinary. You must pick it up from context, or you must ask. Precalibration helps you in an instance like this. When faced with such a situation, precalibrate, and then ask a smart question, such as "How should I address you? I'm not sure." Nonbinary people know this can be confusing to others, and they're prepared to answer this question. Without precalibration, you can easily blunder into the situation and say any number of wrong things.

Something like this happened to me not long ago. My team had received a question from a nonbinary individual who wanted to know whether we could store the proper pronoun in our enterprise data systems. This person had received multiple communications that used the pronoun *she,* which was incorrect. The individual preferred to be referred to as *they.* We needed to communicate back and forth a few times, and I was constantly making the mistake of inserting *she* instead of *they.* When I ultimately needed to communicate to this person and others, I had to precalibrate to ensure that my microcommunications used the correct pronouns.

---

[3] See National Center for Transgender Equality, October 5, 2018, https://transequality.org/issues/resources/understanding-non-binary-people-how-to-be-respectful-and-supportive.

Behavioral Backsliding

One of the reasons I am not suitable for a debate team is that I frequently resort to this argument: "Isn't it obvious?" As it turns out, that isn't really a debate strategy! Few things in the world are manifest, microbehaviors included. Not many of us monitor our behaviors in such minute detail that we're conscious of them on a continuous basis. This suggests we're more capable of forgetting than remembering. I suspect this is due to a misunderstanding about the potential importance of small details.

Let's set out the reasons why we tend to forget, versus remember, the need to dynamically manage our microbehaviors on an ongoing basis.

- We don't realize the potential impact on others, negative or positive.
- We decide the investment is less than the return on investment and just move on.
- We believe that most people ignore them anyway.
- We determine we don't have the proper skills to craft them.
- We've poor memories and tend to lose the past quickly.
- We lack focus and don't know how to improve our attention.

Whatever the reason—and I'm willing to bet there are many more—there's a satisfaction to be gained in being aware enough of a situation or person to intentionally model positive microbehaviors.

2

Microbehavioral Leadership Solutions

Employing the word *solution* in the context of microbehaviors will likely strike you as pretentious. Declaring there is a solution to a problem implies something exact and absolute, such as the solution to the math problem 9 × 6. I learned my multiplication tables in first grade from Mrs. Pine. The answer, of course, is 54. It's a problem that has an exact solution. But in the management sciences, using the word *solution* could be interpreted as "This is the one and only." Let's go instead with *possible solution*.

Alain de Lille said famously that "a thousand roads lead men forever to Rome." While there might not be a thousand roads in the management sciences, there are at least many roads. I've used all types of frameworks and models over four decades of work in leadership development. I like some better than others. All have their charms. Focusing on microbehaviors, both good and bad, is but one road, but it's a useful one to travel.

From where I stand, using appropriate microbehaviors as a tactic is valid up to a certain point. What is that point? Let's say this: microbehaviors keep their utility provided the person sending is objectively, positively intentioned and the person receiving is equipped to interpret the behavior as such. If the receiver can't or doesn't receive positively, then you probably need a different approach that is more precisely tuned to that person's frequency. Strategy A may work for person A splendidly, but for person B, it could be an abject failure.

A few years back, I was attempting to cultivate a relationship with someone I had pegged as an extroverted, intuitive individual who was, I thought, impetuously judgmental. I tried many different tactics appealing to his extroversion and then his intuitive sensibilities. I received in return introverted process behaviors and an inability to decide and commit. I wanted him to sell a product that the team I was financing had recently brought to market. I thought he was the perfect salesman.

I said, "How do you feel about pitching the concept and marketing plan to Walmart? We have the product, but I'd like for them to get excited about the possibilities before they see it." The response I received was something like this: "We need more specific collateral materials before we can talk to them, and I'd really like to do more practicing with smaller retailers before we talk to Walmart. I think we should delay longer and gather more market data." Uh-oh. I had used tried-and-true conversational tactics for extroverted, intuitive people, and nothing had worked.

One day I surprised him by asking him to take a personality assessment. He was puzzled but did it anyway. Guess what. He was an introverted processer with an aversion to decision-making. I had been microbehaviorally misguided.

Microbehaviors shouldn't be relied upon in circumstances where a more comprehensive set of behaviors that play out over time are necessary. A six-month executive coaching program is not a microbehavior, a microintervention, or any other word or tactic you can attach to *micro*. Yet embarking on such could be valid and important in the right context.

On Objectivity and Subjectivity

We've all been in situations where we believe we're being objectively accurate and feel that subjectivity is not playing a meaningful role in our decision-making or advocacy process. I've always thought that being objective was about applying a set of known and agreed-upon data to make an important recommendation or decision. Since objectivity can shift around on any given day, I must be particularly careful that I'm not making up a story in my head that ultimately reflects my personal set of biases. Data helps me to remain objective.

Subjectivity is more about applying one's own view of the world, fortressed upon personal experiences from one's past. It's about making a cognitive leap based on our best guess. Being subjective is about accepting imprecision and favoring intuition. The phrase *eye of the beholder* comes to mind. Margaret Wolfe originally used this phrase in her 1878 novel *Molly Bawn*. The full phrase is "Beauty is in the eye of the beholder." Subjectivity at its best and potentially most meaningful!

I'm bringing up this distinction because both objectivity and subjectivity can be replete with positive intent. How we approach a person, via a microbehavior, is frequently shaped by one or the other. For example:

- Objective, positive intent: "I've seen the report on your sales numbers last month, and I want to heartily congratulate you on a brilliant accomplishment. Thank you for all your efforts."

- Subjective, positive intent: "I've known you for a long time and have seen you succeed in many challenging situations. You'll be able to hit your sales numbers next month; I'm sure of it."

The objective statement is based on a set of data arising from the past. That's what makes it objective. The subjective statement is based on data arising from the past but is entirely based on a set of assumptions. Past performance doesn't imply future success without an intuitive leap being made. You get the idea.

Context Matters

Let's elaborate a bit on the notion of context. Dr. Beau Lotto said, "Context is everything. Your brain doesn't do absolutes. Your brain only does relationships. That's all it ever does and that's all it can ever do." Context gives humans the ability to assign meaning to a person, place, thing, concept, or event. When it comes to microbehaviors, context rules, and facts drool! Raw, disconnected data and information don't create the same emotional punch that context does.

If it rains at the funeral of a dearly departed relative and you're soaked to the skin while standing around the grave in the graying solemnity of a winter afternoon, perhaps only dismal thoughts will come to mind. But if, at the same graveside service, you feel the warmth of the air brushing your cheeks, with the scent of fresh flowers filling your senses, in the brightening light of a spring morning, optimistic thoughts might come to mind instead. Whether rain or shine, your relative is still, sadly, deceased. But in the context of life all around, you will remember the event differently, and you will feel differently in retrospect.

This happened to me. My father, Franklin Artell Smith, died in late December 1976 and was lowered to his final resting place as the sun died in the western sky. A bone-chilling wind swirled around me. There were perhaps twelve people at the grave site. I've nothing but dark memories of that day and the days that followed, which were like photocopies of the day he was buried.

Three decades later, my older brother, Matthew Artell Smith, died in late spring and was lowered down as the sun rose in the sky, with the promise of warmth racing toward me from the east. Many Smith family members were present. I've good memories of that day because of the comfort I felt from those who loved Matt and the context in which the graveside service took place.

Dad and Matt were both gone, and I grieved for them. But the context of their funerals affected me and planted within me very different and somewhat contradictory emotions. The construct of a recipient's context and environment, when you send out a microbehavior, is as important as the words, actions, and messages you intend for the recipient.

We're able to create meaningful, pertinent interpretations of the context in which we find ourselves. It's true we don't always control the constituent parts of context, but we're able to control our reactions to context. The context in which you operate is influenced by others. Seeing through someone else's context is an act of will, not necessarily an intervention in the physical environment. If, in your mind, you overlay context with depressing, annoying, or alarming interpretations— and those are certainly not desirable emotions—you've surrendered control to another person.

When I'm teaching adults in a classroom environment, I try to set out when we're likely to take breaks. This is partly because of the need for people to check in on what's happening back at the office, and I like to give them some comfort that a specific time is planned and will arrive soon. I mostly manage to take breaks every seventy-five minutes of lecture, discussion, or activities. The last comment I make to participants in the class before returning to delivering content is "Suffering is optional." Most people get what I mean.

Suffering *is* optional. In 1903, James Allen published his famous book *As a Man Thinketh*. Many point to Allen's book as the genesis of the self-help movement in the United States. Norman Vincent Peale and Dale Carnegie were influenced by Allen. Plus, we see in the middle of the twentieth century a growing body of literature.

If you're ready to send out a microbehavior, think about the other individuals' context. Are they having a good day or a bad day? Are they anxious or worried? Have they betrayed entirely positive emotions, such as joy, happiness, mirth, or similar? If you can detect the state of mind of others, you can influence their context. For example, if you note the contextual indicators of a bad day, start with a microbehavior. For example, warmly shake the person's hand. Or you can say, "It's been so long, and I'm delighted we can be together." Another possibility would be to start out with deliberate small talk about family or the weather. Recall a positive memory that you share with the person. The person's context will begin to shift, and that will aid you in achieving your communications objectives.

Developing Positive Microbehaviors

Learning about microbehaviors is a way to begin to govern yourself more effectively with a higher degree of positive precision. If you want to be in control, you need to be aware of all the outputs of your verbal interactions, physical movements, and written communications. I've taught many classes where the subject wasn't described as *microbehaviors*, but the concepts were highly aligned.

Think about any personality assessment you may have taken yourself. It could have been the Myers-Briggs Type Indicator (MBTI), DiSC, StrengthsFinder, or any other of the many that are available. Every element of every assessment I've ever used contains a behavioral component. For example, when debriefing the MBTI, I tell participants to start small in order to engineer longer-term change. To an extrovert, I say, "Don't speak first; let others start." To an introvert, I say, "Speak first; don't hang back." Both are microbehavioral encouragements. If these are done over a period consistently, the extrovert and the introvert will meet somewhere in the middle.

Microbehaviors will evolve over time as you positively reinforce the ones that are successful and shun the ones that are not. How long does it take to evolve? That's a great question. We've all heard some rules of thumb to begin to create a timeline of possibility. For example, the 21/90 rule has made its way around for some time. To create a new habit, you need to apply yourself for twenty-one days in a row. To make it a permanent part of your routine, you'll need to continue for ninety days. I've seen this work.

My Mentor and Me

> MENTOR. The interaction I just witnessed between you and Denise wasn't very positive or productive. I worry that your relationship with her is deteriorating.

ARTELL. I think you're right. It's getting worse. Not sure I can turn this around.

MENTOR. Things were going well until you said you didn't trust her most recent hire. Is it true you don't trust him?

ARTELL. Not exactly. I guess I haven't really worked with him enough to know. Are you thinking I need to go make amends somehow?

MENTOR. If you had said to me what you said to Denise, I'm pretty sure I'd have reacted negatively.

ARTELL. This is so hard. Denise and I don't see eye to eye on most things. It feels as if we're working at cross-purposes. I'm upset.

MENTOR. A situation that was made no better when you said, "I don't trust your new hire," right? That *did* upset Denise.

ARTELL. How do I step back from this precipice and make it better?

MENTOR. Start with something simple. For example, apologize, and ask her to meet you over lunch at her favorite place.

ARTELL. I don't think I've ever had lunch, dinner, or any other meal with her. That's a good place to start.

My mentor gave me great advice in this situation. I won't say that my relationship with Denise was completely turned around. We still had our moments, and my mentor needed to occasionally referee. But both of us began to agree to disagree. When it was important that Denise and I reach a consensus, then we got going until we did so.

3

Microbehaviors Get Noticed and Judged

Do you think your behaviors aren't being closely observed by others? I mean all behaviors, at least at work. In a class I teach for new managers, I often say that their employees are continuously watching them, whether they want them to or not. Usually, a few managers say to me that they're not interesting enough to watch, to which I reply, "You can make someone's day go well or poorly. You can be energizing or defeating, happy or sad. Wouldn't an employee find it worthwhile to watch you carefully?" I know I do.

One leader I worked for frequently looked down and away from me or other team members when we walked into his office. That was a sure sign he had something unpleasant to say or discuss. When he maintained eye contact, we all knew the meeting would go better. Such microbehaviors are noticed by employees and acted upon. Managers unintentionally or unconsciously say and do things that are clearly detectable behaviors. Think. When do you know without a doubt it's a good time to speak with your manager? When do you know it's a bad time? Everyone you manage asks the same questions.

Aligning Intentions and Actions

Your employees generally hope for your intentions to match your actions. They look for small signs that alignment is indeed what they're observing and that your intentions are true to your actions. Naturally, employees hope for positive behaviors, and they look keenly for them. If you tell your employees that their opinions count for something, they will be alert for signs of just that.

One manager who reported to me wasn't having much success in conveying to an employee that the person had long-term promotional prospects at the company. I inquired as to what he'd already tried. He said at every opportunity, in every one-on-one conversation, he'd reinforced the high-potential theme. I asked what else he'd considered and was met with silence. Alignment of the manager's intentions and microbehaviors was the situation to be acknowledged. But the overall microbehavioral landscape was insufficient for the needs of the high-potential employee. Adjustments and expansions were required.

I asked whether the employee could be invited to our department's leadership team meeting to report on a particularly important project. Yes, he could. I asked whether the employee could perhaps accompany us to an outside community event next month. Yes, he could. These were simple, intentional microbehaviors that would count for good in the mind of the employee. Note that this isn't how I'd approach a long-term development plan for the employee. Yet the microbehaviors did demonstrate alignment with intentions and language in the short term.

What's a microbehavioral landscape? In the story above, the employee had heard from the manager but hadn't heard from anyone else, including the one-up manager, me. The landscape he detected was one of confidentiality, privacy, and secrecy. One voice is important, but a landscape that doesn't include one other living person is barren at the outset.

I've found that many organizations are reluctant to say to an employee, "You're high-potential, and we want you to be successful." I think managers are reticent because they can't by themselves create a more conducive environment. High-potentials need investment and publicity more broadly, across team, department, and enterprise. There might be one other reason. If managers are not designated as high-potentials, they may withhold because they themselves are not receiving much TLC.

One possible way to combat this phenomenon is to ask managers to present to you the full team and listen to their assessment of each employee, including high-potentials. The process of candid discussion allows you to influence and coach as appropriate. The process also creates better alignment with the managers' own perspectives and potentially opens the door to a developmental conversation with the managers. Every employee, high-potential or not, has an expectation of development and generally relishes personal conversations with his or her manager. Of course, the managers must be in control of their microbehaviors!

Helping Others through Microbehavioral Management

Despite the obvious fact that you're the one demonstrating the microbehaviors, your behaviors should not be designed to benefit only you. "What?" you say. "Where is the enlightened self-interest? What of positioning yourself positively and agreeably for others to remark upon?" As in the example above of the employee I invited to the leadership team meeting, others may have thought of me as generous and perhaps insightful. My efforts at microinclusion for the high-potential employee were intended for the employee alone, to reinforce, in a small way, the company's intentions toward him.

To be truly successful in the business of helping others, you'll need to have some relevant tools in your kit bag. The example above about the high-potential employee suggests that the manager may have benefitted from a few additional tactics or techniques. Some things that could've helped the manager include the following: knowledge of the 70/20/10 rule of development; command of *Six Conversations* and *Brag, Worry, Wonder, Bet*; grasp of personality types and styles; and appreciation of what it takes to connect fully with high-potentials. The 70/20/10 rule is aimed at how managers consider an employee's development within the company: 70 percent of that development occurs through on-the-job training, 20 percent occurs through one-on-one training with an expert, and 10 percent occurs through in-class formal training.

While it's critical for your microbehaviors to positively impact others, well-placed and well-timed microbehaviors can create happy by-products for you as well. Are you seen as grumpy and distant at work? A microbehavior that includes a smile, and a personal comment can change that perception. Or are you likely to interrupt others at team meetings, potentially closing conversation before it even starts? An open-ended question inviting others to speak first can go a long way toward establishing your interest in the opinions of others.

In the end, leaders and managers are judged in the harsh light of day for both small things and big things, which I discussed in the preface. If you walk into a room full of your fellow employees, immediately rush to speak with the boss, and then depart, what will others think of that? It's a microbehavior in the sense of being observed for a short period of time, with little context related to what you said to the boss or what she said back.

Anyone who observes the behavior described above could view it in at least two ways. The first way could be like this: "He only wants to be seen by the boss and doesn't care about the rest of us." The second way could be like this: "He must have something really important going on, because he didn't get a chance to say hello to us." Validity of the judgment made is in the eye of the beholder, and one or the other judgment could pop out based on prior microbehaviors. It's all related.

Your Worldview and Microbehaviors

I've traveled to India quite a few times on business. My first trip to Delhi was a bit unnerving. While I knew in concept what I'd see and hear, I didn't prepare adequately for the actual experience. We landed in the middle of the night and were driven to an expensive hotel that catered to Westerners. It was very hot and muggy, and there were many new smells. The hotel staff knew what they were doing. As much as possible, they kept us in a Western-feeling bubble. Everyone spoke English, and we were handed ice-cold bottled water. The hotel itself was open, light, and cool. It was everything a Westerner could want. We were quickly ushered to our rooms and went to bed.

By morning, my worldview was already changing. On the car ride to the office, it changed further as I took in the sights, sounds, and smells of this new country. It was overwhelming at first, but the newness of the experience pushed me to look at the world around me in a different way, one that was much more open to concepts and ideas that never had occurred to me before.

When we arrived at the office, the local general manager, Sanjeev, greeted us and showed us to seats in his office. Sanjeev must have noticed I was a bit pale, because he looked me square in the eye and said, "You need to remember that there are more than one billion of us, Artell. We're everywhere. You'll get used to it." He was right. I did eventually get used to India, and my worldview was permanently changed. For example, I could never again look at poverty in the United States in the same way. Seeing starvation up close, as I did in India, was transformative and unsettling, prompting me to be more aware and empathetic.

One reason for my worldview shift was driven by India's population, as foreshadowed above. India is a country of huge proportions. From a population density perspective, India has roughly 1,202 people per square mile, while the United States has 94 people per square mile. There are different ways to calculate population density, so I invite you to look it up for more precise numbers.

Specifically, my worldview changed in the way I perceive how the Western countries contemplate India or most of the continent of Africa. It's a narrow conception, of which I was also guilty. The vibrancy of life in India was breathtaking. The bright colors that were common components of dress of both women and men changed my attitude of what is acceptable or desirable in the workplace. I had tremendous appreciation for the hard work that many had to do to keep themselves and their families healthy and thriving. On my return trips to Chicago, I always felt that something was missing when I deplaned into the cavernous, never-ending hallways and thoroughfares in O'Hare. I missed India.

I'm over sixty years old now, and some of my worldview is based on the era in which I grew up. As a teenager in upstate

New York during the 1970s, I picked up an interesting behavior. During the oil crisis of late 1973 and early 1974, I recall driving around town with my mother in a huge Plymouth station wagon, looking for a place to buy gasoline. Mom was crying, something she rarely did, out of frustration that no place we went was open. The Plymouth's gas tank was nearly empty. She made an offhand comment about how she shouldn't have let it get under half a tank.

That was all it took. To this day, I get anxious when the gas-tank level reaches half, and I start looking for a station to fill up. It doesn't matter if I have enough gas for two hundred miles or more; I stop to get gas automatically. Why? Because gas is a scarce resource already on the planet, and it could suddenly be in short supply.

Worldview-Driven Microbehaviors

If you come from a Christian background, you likely think of December as the Christmas holiday month, and you're likely to say, "Merry Christmas," to many people, even those who don't celebrate. You're not necessarily wrong, but it's also the month when Jewish people celebrate Hanukkah (depending on the year) and when many in the black community celebrate Kwanzaa. Let's not forget that December 10 is Human Rights Day, and December 15 is Bill of Rights Day—also good reasons to celebrate. My point is this: be sure to check your microbehaviors and not assume everybody is interested in the same things you are. A "Happy holidays!" greeting or "Good to see you!" may serve you better in December.

Here's another worldview-driven microbehavior I've become sensitized to at work. It's typical in meetings to designate a notetaker. This is true whether you operate in a virtual, physical, or hybrid environment. Let's say you're leading the meeting. How do you determine who'll be asked to take notes and keep track of action items? It's a clerical function, and women, in your worldview, could be identified with these tasks. So, do you usually ask a woman in the meeting to take notes? I've heard from many women that they experience this. How about a new microbehavior? Rotate the responsibility, rather than relying on the women in the group. Men and women can share equally. Oh, and don't forget to take a turn yourself! This and many other stereotypes should be jettisoned from the workplace, and all microbehaviors attached to them should cease.

Examining Your Worldview

If I stop to really consider what my worldview is, I come up with a few obvious and a few surprising things. I hale from a conservative, religious background, though I'm no longer very religious. My education was at a church-sponsored institution, and most of my career has been in large, mostly conservative organizations. Along the way, I've been in almost every job there is within HR. I've defined myself in terms of what I can do to help people, especially in the context of a values-driven organization as expressed through people processes. But I'm decidedly much more liberal than either of my parents and any of my siblings or other relatives. The few people I've kept in touch with from graduate school are multiple standard deviations more conservative than I am.

Upon introspection, I'm pretty sure I know why my worldview has shifted so dramatically. I think it's because I've lived many places across the United States since high school, worked for several multinational companies, and spent a fair amount of time traveling to places around the world. I've also moved far away from the high-demand religion I grew up with.

My two grown sons have greatly influenced me as well. Here are the elements of my current worldview:

- People usually try to do the right thing but sometimes fail.
- People should be held accountable for their misdeeds.
- People aren't the same, and differences should be honored.
- Spirituality springs from within and is demonstrated in many forms.
- Life is short, so don't waste your time on doing things you don't like.
- Education is critical, and people need curiosity to survive.
- For good reason, we should be suspicious of big institutions.
- Family traditions have meaning, but don't follow them blindly.
- Don't worry about having lots of friends, just good friends.

As I said, I've lived all over the United States, including New York, New Jersey, Virginia, Florida, Texas, Utah, Ohio, Illinois, and Wisconsin. I've also visited a few other countries, including Canada, the United Kingdom, France (where I lived for two years), Spain, India, Denmark, Iceland, Belgium, and Scotland. I speak both English and French, and I'm learning Spanish. Taken all together, I know I've adjusted my worldview over time, learned to be more tolerant, and developed a craving for the perspectives of outsiders. Knowing all these things about myself helps me to create contextually correct and appropriate microbehaviors. Sometimes I get it wrong, but I'm improving.

I know there are some things that are too personal to talk about to others. Perhaps aspects of your worldview fall into the only-you category. To the extent you have aspects of the real you to share, I'd encourage you to do so. The reason, of course, is that a goodly number of your microbehaviors spring from both your past experiences and your worldview.

Growing up in the Northeast meant snowstorms by Halloween and sometimes on Easter Sunday. Being the son of two research chemists meant I never had a chance to learn or appreciate anything related to sports, but I did learn a lot about classical music. I have microbehaviors related to snow and snow removal—including a propensity to walk by snowblowers in every store where they're sold to check them out. I also have microbehaviors related to classical music—including a strong desire to talk about and listen to the fourth movement of Brahms's Symphony no. 1 (don't ask).

Worldview microbehaviors, as we've been discussing, go even deeper and therefore need some additional explanation to others. Because I lived in France and speak French—something not obvious when you look at me—I sometimes will suddenly use a French phrase, such as "*Mon Dieu. Quelle horreur!*" (My God. What a horror!) or "You can't keep them on the farm once they've seen Paris." I don't say that phrase in French, but I still get a look when I use it. Other microbehaviors go deeper still.

Above, I mentioned that my worldview includes deep suspicion of big institutions. A frequent microbehavior related to this worldview is that I'll avoid walking into government buildings or interacting with the government at all levels. Right after I received my master of public administration, I was offered a prestigious Presidential Management Internship working for the federal government. I didn't take it. But why am I so attracted to working for big companies? I'm not. I'm attracted to interesting, complex work, and big companies are where such work is frequently found. When in a large company, I'll make friends with relatively few people and work with them as much as possible.

Appreciative Inquiry and Generativity

Later, I'll discuss microrecognition, microcompliments, and micromotivation. I'd like to preview here two concepts that are pertinent to our mindset discussions: appreciative inquiry and generativity.

Quickly defined, appreciative inquiry is a process that enables you to build relationships more effectively using positive, affirming words, and questioning techniques. Generativity takes a little longer to define, and it has a very specific meaning.

Erik Erikson and Gordon Flett proposed definitions for *generativity*. For specifics, see Flett's book *The Psychology of Mattering* (2018). In brief, generativity is the ability and willingness of older adults to promote the well-being of younger generations. It could be someone in middle age helping a twentysomething, or it could be a sixtysomething helping a fortysomething. To be successful in such endeavors, your mindset needs to include the beliefs that the long-term survival of the species matters, and that younger people need to be fostered and encouraged.

When you were a younger version of yourself—perhaps during the early part of your career—did you have someone in your life who went out of his or her way to teach you and help you develop? I had a few, and I bet you did too. In the Preface, I mentioned one of my mentors, Steve King. But there were others who showed me the way. One of my managers at the financial services company noticed me and started to take an interest in my development. I'm a late-generation boomer, and my manager, Serena, was a midgeneration boomer. Serena was already a senior vice president when I met her, and I was a new director. This leader had a hand in hiring me, and I continue to be appreciative to her for that.

In my first year as a director, Serena gave me a meaty project whose purpose was to create an educational program for trainers to develop facilitation skills. At the end of the project, Serena promoted me to vice president and asked me to move to Boston. I'm eight years younger than Serena, and I quickly realized the promotion and move were acts of generativity. She cared about those who were earlier in their careers and was prompted to develop them. I was a grateful recipient of her wise counsel and coaching. In part because of Serena's generativity, since that time, I've also paid close attention to the rising generations under my care who likewise need help and guidance—so much so that it has become a permanent part of my mindset.

Now we're back where we started at the beginning of this chapter, namely a change in mindset created by environmental factors and lived experiences. We all need to be open to such possibilities. I'm not someone who believes that everything happens for a reason, but I'm someone who believes that intentional reasoning brings about everything that happens.

4

Microbehaviors and Diversity, Equity, and Inclusion

Since the murder of George Floyd on May 25, 2020, I've spent a significant amount of time in study and contemplation about diversity, equity, and inclusion (DEI). Diversity work isn't new to me. I've been attached to aspects of DEI since graduate school. The companies I've worked for all had DEI programmatic offerings. At the major oil company I worked for in the early 1990s, I went through my first diversity sensitivity class. The conversations in the class were a bit puzzling to me. They were so obvious. And I was the most junior person in the room. After the class, upon returning to the office, I couldn't help but observe that there were no further discussions, and nothing changed.

In a random meeting I attended soon after the workshop, the topic of diversity recruiting came up. My role in HR at that point was as a compensation specialist in a research facility, and one of my daily tasks was to create the pay offers for new recruits. My manager, who was very woke, was discussing the company's lack of diversity and strategies we could employ to improve the situation.

The COO of the subdivision said, "I think it's normal that a manager would only want to hire people who look like him."

Oh, I see, I thought. We only had white managers. The expression on my face betrayed my emotion, and I got *the look* from my manager seated across the table, which said clearly, "Don't say anything right now." For the record, seventeen words in the COO's sentence and four seconds to deliver them represented a microbehavior that had a huge negative impact on me. Which other senior leaders believed that? I wondered.

We adjourned the meeting, and I followed my manager to her office. She said to me, "The COO is never going to change his ways, and we have to wait until he retires next year." I accepted the answer eventually, with the hope that there would be a difference in the future. I was transferred to another affiliate about six months later and never heard anything more.

Understanding Microaggressions

For a formal definition of *microaggression*, I like this one: a microaggression is an intentional or unintentional verbal or nonverbal slight, snub, or affront that transmits uncomplimentary, hostile, and negative messages to members of a stigmatized or marginalized group. Chester Pierce, a black Harvard-trained psychiatrist, was the first to describe these acts as microaggressions in the 1960s.

For clarity and for consistency with common current practice within the DEI community, *microaggression* is uniquely applied to marginalized communities. The term is not applied to dominant community members. When I use the phrase *nondominant communities*, I'm referring to stigmatized or marginalized groups. *Dominant* may not always be the appropriate designation, and I think you should consider which word—perhaps *centralized*—might serve you better. The specific situation will guide you to the right language.

I can't remember the first time I heard the word *microaggression* said out loud, but I read about it in the book *Inclusive Conversations* by Mary-Frances Winters. In chapter 11 of her book, titled "Mind Your Words," Mary-Frances discusses the importance of word choice, and the way words can be used like weapons if you're not careful. Mary-Frances goes quite a bit further down the road of microaggressions, including a great discussion on how to combat them. I recommend *Inclusive Conversations* to you and hope you'll read it.

The definition of *microaggression*, though short, is multifaceted. The analysis of microaggressions is frequently an eye-of-the-beholder exercise simply because something that is aggressive or offensive to one disenfranchised community might not be aggressive or offensive to another or to the dominant community. By way of an example, I'm chagrined to say that I've personally used the word *powwow* at work when referring to a meeting: "We need a powwow to strategize how to find talent in the New York market." The meaning of *powwow* is plain enough. I can't count how many times I've heard it used in just this way.

But the use of *powwow* is likely a microaggression, and you shouldn't use it at all, unless you have a cultural connection to indigenous peoples in North America. The word derives from *pau wau*, which means "medicine man" In Narrtick, a language spoken by the Algonquian peoples in what is now Massachusetts. English settlers co-opted the phrase and started to use it in the wrong way, and that's how we got here. Unless you've a legitimate reason to describe a meeting of medicine men, don't use *powwow*.

My mother started her career in academia in 1964. She was appointed assistant professor of chemistry at Russell Sage College in Troy, New York, having completed her PhD at Rutgers in 1960. Mom was a pioneer in many ways, and she was a feminist. I'm grateful to Mom for teaching me some basic lessons about equality and equity.

While I won't go into the history of women's colleges in the United States, suffice it to say that Russell Sage was one. In 1964, there were no male students on campus in Troy. I heard from Mom more than once a story like this: "I can't believe Dr. [Male Faculty] still refers to Sage as a girls' school! Doesn't seem to matter how many times I correct them; they still say it." At first, I was confused. I was a boy. The students at Sage were girls. What was the big deal? I clearly didn't get it.

Mom didn't use the word *microaggression*, though that was what it was—a microaggression directed toward women, whether faculty members or students, in the prevalent context of women in higher education, who were historically a stigmatized and marginalized group. Mom would patiently explain to me—and it took more than one time—that men and women went to college, not boys and girls. You can get away with *boys* and *girls* when you're talking about high school or lower grade levels but not college. Is a twenty-two-year-old woman about to graduate with a degree in chemistry a girl? Hardly.

When I asked her who called Sage a girls' school, she responded that only the male faculty members and men outside the college used that term. Why did the male faculty members and others persist? I wish I knew the answer. The *boys* kept saying it, and it irritated Mom. Were they really that unobservant of the women around them? The answer is no, they weren't unobservant. But they didn't care much either. This microaggression perpetuated by many male faculty members went on for most of the sixteen years Mom was at Sage. When she became a full professor, the chemistry department chair, the dean of faculty, and then the academic dean, they said it a lot less frequently!

I occasionally hear from dominant group members that they're surprised at the strength of reaction from a stigmatized or marginalized group member because of a microaggression. In fact, dominant group members are generally a little slow to realize that a statement, comment, word, picture, context, or story could be a microaggression or even an aggression.

For example, do you know what WLM means? White Lives Matter. Using WLM is an act of aggression toward the marginalized black community, in my opinion. The three words by themselves don't seem too far out of bounds, except that WLM is a white-supremacist phrase that originated in early 2015 as a racist response to the BLM—Black Lives Matter—movement. You can Google the history of WLM and see for yourself the racist intentions associated with the phrase. I'd say that using WLM in any situation is always a microaggression, and probably something much worse.

There is a potentiality of any demographic group's name being placed before *lives matter*. What does that mean in terms of whether the new three-word result is a microaggression, an aggression, or no aggression at all? I'm not smart enough to understand all the ramification of this possibility. Many variations could coexist with Black Lives Matter—for example, Women's Lives Matter, Gay Lives Matter, Latinx Lives Matter, Asian Lives Matter, and more. I would submit that the analysis must turn on whether the phrase has a xenophobic origin intended to tear down or harm. Such complexities need to be worked out as we move forward into a more inclusive world.

It's important to understand that marginalized peoples and communities are constantly exposed to microaggressions.

Microaggressions against the Marginalized

Let's look at one more example of a microaggression in a DEI context. I've a good friend who is a member of the LGBTQIA+ community, a cisgender gay white male. He recounted a story to me about a "joke" another employee made about how busy the men's restroom was at an off-site conference. The straight white male employee said to my gay colleague that he could always go to the women's restroom instead of the men's, since it wasn't crowded.

Just in case my description isn't crisp enough, how about this?

"Look how crowded the men's room is! People are lining up outside the door."

"Yes but look over there; the women's room is empty. You could use the women's room, right? The women won't worry about you being there!"

Oh dear. How incredibly ignorant. How's this funny? If you had been in the position of my gay friend, what would you have done? Well, having experienced this kind of potty humor before, he just laughed and moved on. Then he called me and asked what I thought he should do. My response was "Go back to the straight guy and tell him exactly what you think. Or I'd be happy to do it." He went and handled it on his own.

Seriously, where does this sort of microaggression come from? I suggest you go back and reread the worldview chapter. Someone in this bigoted person's past likely made a negative reference, or a series of them, about gay men, and over a period, it emboldened this straight male to perpetuate that negative worldview. I'd say he needs a quick awakening and a fast trip to a different state of mind.

Microaggression versus Aggression

In the section above, I proposed that potty humor was a microaggression. In my current view, based on my continuing journey toward understanding, I'd classify it now as an aggression. It might be a good idea to refresh ourselves on the differences between the two types of hurtful or hateful communications between dominant and nondominant culture members.

Aggression Characteristics	Microaggression Characteristics

• An overt insult, delivered by a dominant group member, designed to intentionally psychologically injure a nondominant or marginalized group member(s).
 	
  o "The HBCUs are not a good talent pool for us, even though we've had some success, like Jamal here. But *he* fits in at the company."
 	
• A purposeful off-color joke, story, or anecdote, delivered by a dominant group member, designed to intentionally psychologically injure a nondominant or marginalized group member(s).
 	
  o "Did you notice the winners at the employee talent show? They were dancing around the stage like they owned the place. No surprise they won. Did you also notice all the judges were gay too? We'll stop this next year."
	• A subtle putdown, possibly unintentional, delivered by a dominant group member to a nondominant or marginalized group member(s).
	
	  o "You're so smart and articulate! I'm glad we set aside our doubts and started recruiting at Morehouse College."
	
	• An attempted joke or supposedly humorous story or anecdote delivered by a dominant group member that's told at the expense of a nondominant or marginalized group member(s).
	
	  o "Did you notice at the employee talent show that first, second, and third place all went to someone in the LGBTQIA+ business resource group? And that they were all dancing and singing numbers? Figures! Of course, I'm joking. They're very talented."

- An intentional statement, delivered by a dominant group member, whose sole purpose is to minimize, invalidate, or eradicate the distinctiveness of a marginalized group member(s).
  - "Most of the Mexicans I know want to assimilate into US culture as quickly as possible. From now on, we'll only hire Mexicans who already speak English. We're not going to pay them to learn English; they must do that on their own."

- A comment, story, or anecdote, delivered by dominant group member, that attempts to invalidate the lived experiences and lifestyle of marginalized group member(s).
  - "We should really help Hispanics to learn English and only speak English at work. They're here in our country, and learning English is a small price to pay. I bet Spanish will eventually just die out in the United States."

There is much more we could explore in terms of examples of both aggressions and microaggressions. The possibilities in the table above could be broadly classified as microinsults, microinvalidations, or microassaults. If you want to research more about these unsavory and insulting communications, you'll find that they span the spectrum of racism, gender sexism, misogyny, heterosexism, transsexism, and many other categories. You need to be aware of what these sound like, so you can cut them off as quickly as possible or address them after the fact. Either way, you should monitor, and be prepared to adjust, your microbehaviors accordingly.

In our day and age, we must be attentive to what we say and how we say it. Race relations in the United States are at an inflection point. I can't recall a time in my life when I've been witness to so many microaggressions and aggressions directed toward marginalized communities. It's reprehensible.

In speaking to a job candidate I was interviewing a few years ago, I asked this question: "Why do you think there are so few black and Latinx managers in most business settings?"

The response was immediate: "They don't want to work hard enough to be managers."

Not certain I'd heard correctly, I went a little further: "Do you mean that black and Latinx individuals aren't clear about what they need to do to become managers?"

The response, again, was immediate: "No, they just don't want it enough and aren't willing to put in the effort."

I couldn't believe my ears. We spoke a bit more, and it was clear he not only had a distinct worldview but also was willing to spout this nonsense. He displayed zero thought before speaking and zero self-awareness.

Understanding Mansplaining

Women also are the recipients of numerous microaggressions, even now in the second fifth of the twenty-first century. One of my female acquaintances described to me what it's like to be the victim of mansplaining.

Is *mansplaining* a new term for you? Maybe it is if you're a man. This is a conversational situation in which a relatively straightforward concept seems to require extensive explanation from a man to a woman. In specific, it's done in a perceived condescending and patronizing way. The thought that any man would take it upon himself to mansplain to a woman is beyond my comprehension. Someone should try mansplaining to my mother. I saw my father do it once or twice. That was fun to watch!

Promoting Allyship

Allyship, especially from dominant group members, demands much. When I first went to college, I had a roommate who was Jewish. His name was Marc, and he was from Utica, New York. I learned a lot from him about Jewish faith and practices. Marc invited me to his home for Passover. I experienced as genuine a Passover celebration as I'm likely to ever experience outside of Israel.

Marc's parents told me stories from their family history that involved World War II and the Holocaust. When discrimination increased significantly against Jewish Americans in 2019 and 2020, I was prepared to say what was needed in any negative or bigoted conversation aimed against those who are Jewish. I describe myself as an ally to those who are Jewish, and my ears are tuned to negative comments about them. My goal, with the help of others, is to be the best ally possible. We can all manifest positive microbehaviors to combat the negativity that surrounds us.

Some of my examples above may seem to you to be outside of anything you might personally say or do—misogynistic comments to women, mansplaining, racial stereotyping, or anti-Semitic remarks. Too much? Unlikely? I'd invite you to think again. Perhaps it's not within your makeup to be overt or intentional. But recall the microinstant of thinking needed to precalibrate your behavior. That's what we need to do to avoid bad behaviors. It can happen very fast. Here are examples of negative microaggressions that can easily slip out.

To Women	1. How many children do you have? And you're pregnant! Must be hard to balance work and family. How do you manage?
	2. You're the first woman on the board of directors. I'm glad they finally decided to take the plunge.
	3. How are you going to keep all those men in line on the maintenance crew? They're tough cookies, but they know their stuff. Don't get too worried about the things they say. They grew up in a different time, you know?
To Blacks	1. Such a cool hairstyle! I don't know anyone else who would do that. Can I touch it?
	2. Should we all have lunch at the country-western bar? Oh, wait—will you feel comfortable there? Probably not your kind of music.
	3. Legend and Princeton? Those are your sons' names? They sound like nicknames! I bet they'll be embarrassed.
To Latinx	1. Have you spoken to the Argentines? You've probably a lot in common, and it'd make them feel better. I know you're from Peru.
	2. Since you're Catholic, what's Midnight Mass like? I've never been. Does it get spooky in the church, just using candles for lighting?
	3. Cinque de Mayo is a big holiday for you at home, isn't it? Let's go out and celebrate. First beer on me!

	4. Wow, you're looking great today, *chiquita*. See? I've learned a little Spanish!
	5. You grew up in Indianapolis? But where are you from originally?
To Muslims	1. I heard you guys don't drink. Is that real or just what people say?
	2. Those Saudi Arabian princes! They're not friends to the United States. Where are you from again? California? Right, but what country did you come from?
	3. Do you consider yourself black or Muslim? Or both?
	4. What holidays do your people celebrate? Not Thanksgiving, I bet!
To Asians	1. Did you have any relatives in the World War II detention camps? Oh, you're Korean? I thought for sure you were Japanese.
	2. What restaurant do you recommend around here for great sushi?
	3. Didn't your brother marry a white girl? What did your parents think about that?
To the Jewish	1. H-a-n-a-k-a? That's how it's spelled, I think. Every other way seems wrong.
	2. What's your rabbi's name? No, his actual name. What does he do when he's not being a rabbi?
	3. We've something in common! A bat mitzvah is just like a quinceañera! I bet both girls will even wear the same kind of fancy dresses. Rosario's will be in brilliant white.

There's a final aspect of microaggressions I want to explore before we close this chapter. A possibility exists that someone could observe you and another person in conversation. Conversing with someone you know well, either from the same or a different cultural background, might be at best confusing or at worst insulting, depending on the subject matter of the conversation. There are many possible scenarios here but consider this interaction with my mentor.

MENTOR. You said you'd overheard a conversation in which more than one of the individuals speaking were using the N-word. Right?

ARTELL. Yes. It was after hours, and there were two black female employees and one biracial male employee talking. They were laughing and joking around, and I tried not to eavesdrop, since it seemed to be a personal, nonwork conversation.

MENTOR. So, the three of them were in friendly conversation while you were in their vicinity?

ARTELL. There were no raised or angry voices. There was a lot of laughing, and they appeared to be enjoying themselves.

MENTOR. Well, we received a complaint about the interaction. Turns out they did know one another, the two black women especially, but they had only recently met the biracial male. Someone else—a different black woman who didn't know any of the three—observed them talking and thought the male was inappropriately using the N-word and was in fact a white guy.

ARTELL. Oh dear. That's a problem. Did someone explain to her what was happening and why it wasn't a problem?

MENTOR. Yes, but the black woman is not backing down from her accusation of a hostile work environment and wants to talk to you since you also observed the conversation. You can probably straighten it out, but she's adamant.

ARTELL. I'll do my best.

MENTOR. We'll probably have to connect the person making the complaint with the two black women and the biracial man. Maybe you and I can learn something in the process.

With only a few variations to protect those involved, the scenario above actually happened. It felt way above my pay grade. I learned a lot by being part of the various interactions after the event was reported.

Microaggressions versus Appropriate Comments

There are two sides we need to examine to determine whether a comment is being received as a microaggression, as in the example above. I need to acknowledge first that the sender's attitude, comportment, intentions, tone, pace, and word choice are not my primary concern. Does it matter in the end if the sender's intentions were pure and devoid of bias? Maybe, or maybe not. I frequently think of the following phrase in my attempt to deconstruct any given interaction: "Ignorance of the law is no excuse." This is an ancient concept tracing back to the Romans and even the Greeks. Thomas Jefferson famously expanded the phrase when he suggested that if one could be excused for ignorance, there would be no compulsion to obey any law.

I've read in several articles and books recently that black people in the United States should not shoulder the burden of explaining their history to white people, meaning white people should do their own research and self-educate when it comes to black history and current conditions. I believe this, and it's critical to understand that this concept applies to all cultures about which you may know little. Ignorance is not a defense when it comes to microaggressions. This is my point of view, and you may disagree. No problem.

Riddle me this: What's the appropriateness of referring to all Latinx people as Mexicans? I've heard explanations like this: "Oh, *Mexicans* is the word I use to refer to everyone who came from south of the US border. I don't mean anything bad by it." Sigh. White people in the United States have been known to get upset when someone fails to accurately name the state, the part of the state, or even the zip code they live in. Imagine the feeling Latinx individuals have when they receive a microaggression declaring that it doesn't matter which of the thirty-three Central American, South American, and Caribbean countries they hale from? Such a declaration is wrong, discourteous, minimizing, and a microaggression.

Imagine two groups of new Latinx employees join a company, representing two different countries, Honduras and Ecuador. These two countries are separated by about 1,300 miles, with at least four other countries in between. Is it possible there are some commonly held cultural customs between the two groups? Sure. But you shouldn't assume that to be the case.

Instead, sit down with employees from each group, and ask questions about their backgrounds and experience. Share your background too. Exhibit curiosity, indicating that you're trying and that you care. You'll soon realize that there are large cultural differences and that each group speaks a version of Spanish with some country-specific vocabulary. Americans don't study in any detail in most high schools the differences between countries in Central and South America. Please don't make up a story that has no basis in fact.

Ignorance is not an excuse. Educate yourself. This is one of the best defenses against blundering into microaggressions.

5

Negative Microbehaviors and Dominant Groups

Let's tackle the issue of microaggression vis-à-vis nonmarginalized or dominant groups. Is it appropriate to use the term *microaggression* in this case? The short answer is no, it's not appropriate. We should reserve *microaggression* for situations where individuals from nondominant, stigmatized, marginalized groups are being targeted. I admit this could be debatable. Yet DEI experts raise a valid issue when it comes to pinpointing microaggressions as pertaining to specific communities: blacks, Latinx, Asians, indigenous peoples, LGBTQIA+, and so forth.

What term should we use then? A few possibilities include *microaffront*, *micro-offense*, *microdisparagement*, *microdefamation*, and *microinsult*. They will all work in this context, namely, to describe a communication that is blatantly uncomplimentary, hostile, and negative and designed to injure the person. Since this book is about microbehaviors, we need to cover openly and with precision what this means.

If I say to a cisgender straight white male, "You're incompetent, and I don't want you to attend these project meetings," I think it's fair to say that the words themselves are intended to injure the person. If I say this in front of others, the injury intended is worse. Is it a microinsult? Yes, at least. Microdefamation? Possibly. But in the meaning of the definitions we've been using, it's not a microaggression. A dominant group member can be subject to a negative microbehavior, which can sting significantly. It's just not a microaggression.

"You shouldn't feel like that! I didn't intend it that way." Famous last words! I wish I could say I've never had to mount this defense after putting my foot in my mouth with a negative microbehavior. I recall with unhappiness one situation in which I said something I immediately regretted. It pains me just to put it down in writing, but I've grown a lot since then, and it makes the point.

I was in a meeting that wasn't going well, in my opinion. There were two other people in the room, but I was only speaking to one of them, and the conversation was getting heated. I looked at the second person, thinking he really didn't need to stay, and I used the phrase "You're dismissed" when asking him to leave. Oh Lord. That was an awful negative microbehavior. Was the person insulted by my unnecessarily harsh language? Yes. Was I embarrassed? Yes. I knew right away that I needed to do something to make amends, and I did, in an HR office with my HR business partner and the employee. Yup, it was that bad.

One additional note about the negative microbehavior example above before we move on. Recall the comments I made about context in chapter 2. If you've been in the military or a high-control environment of any kind, using the word *dismissed* may not hit you the same way. If you've heard *dismissed* twenty times in a day and it signaled only "Time to leave," would you be insulted?

Here's the experience you need to understand. In my time at the major oil company, which preceded the incident, three of my four managers were military academy graduates: two were West Point, and one was Coast Guard Academy. All were white males. Did they say to me, "You're dismissed," when it was time for me to leave a room or meeting? You betcha. But for the person I said *dismissed* to in the meeting, it was a microaggression—not his context at all.

It's not always that simple or obvious. In a SWOT[4] workshop I was invited to attend once, I was puzzled at the slow pace of the session. For those who are unfamiliar with SWOT, it's a structured team interaction in which team members set out their current circumstances (situation), their developmental needs (weaknesses), their hoped-for accomplishments (opportunities), and their upcoming or existing challenges that might slow the team down (threats), hence the acronym SWOT.

At any rate, I noticed the session was going slowly. I'd worked with the subject matter experts in attendance for about six months. I knew they could move faster, and I'd seen them do so in other settings. I raised my hand and asked, "Is there any way we can move through this preliminary material faster?" I thought it was an innocent question, though I probably said those words with a bit of my characteristic impatient edge.

The facilitator, a former employee of the company who had been engaged to run the workshop, flushed red. As Scooby-Doo said, my only thought was *Ruh-roh*. Back and forth we went. Temperatures started to rise, and others began

---

[4] SWOT stands for "situation, weakness, opportunity, threat." Also see the glossary for a definition.

to jump in. A guy from New York said he felt uncomfortable and wanted us to stop. New York! I looked around for support from others in the room on trying to push things faster. Guess what. No support. None. Nada. I'd really stepped in it.

All told, there were maybe three minutes of repartee—microaggression territory. We took a break. I started apologizing, especially to the facilitator. Some were ready to forgive—others not so much. The facilitator wasn't happy with me at all. He said I'd been against him from the start. That was an exaggeration, but I decided retreat was the best option, and I beat a hasty one.

To the collective relief of the participants, I found other things to do that day. I was eventually invited back. When I asked someone later about the incident, he said, "Your question was disrespectful toward the process. You should've demonstrated more trust." I thanked him for his advice and resolved to do better.

My Mentor and Me

MENTOR. Is that really what happened? Did you say that to the facilitator of the SWOT session?

ARTELL. I'm not proud of it.

MENTOR. You could make further amends if you want to. It was harsh. As a facilitator, you know how vulnerable you can be when in front of a classroom.

ARTELL. Yes, sir. But what can I do now? I think I apologized enough to the actual facilitator in the story.

MENTOR. How about this? Why don't you discuss briefly what you should've done to understand better what was happening in the SWOT session? You know, instead of disrupting the whole thing and causing a ruckus.

ARTELL. I like the way you're thinking! OK, I do have some ideas. Let me go through three that come to mind. I'm going to concentrate on microbehavior options:

1) At any time before the meeting, I could've asked the facilitator, "What can I do to help you on the day of the workshop? I'm happy to do whatever is needed."

2) At any time before the meeting, I could've said to any company manager or leader who had gone through the company's SWOT protocol, "I'm not familiar with how this will all play out, though I know the objectives of the workshop. What can I expect, and how can I support it?"

3) During the meeting, at the point when I was beginning to get frustrated with the overall pace, I could've waited for the next break and asked the person sitting next to me, "What's your feeling about how things are going? Are we making the right progress in your mind?"

MENTOR. What I especially like about the three options is that none of them include you going up to the facilitator and messing with the plan he had made for the day, which someone must have approved at the company. Is that right?

ARTELL. Yes, 100 percent. All the right leaders had approved the workshop, its objectives, and how it was going to run. I wasn't part of that process.

MENTOR. It was hard to undo what you said to the facilitator, wasn't it?

ARTELL. Oh yeah. Definitely. It never really was the same with some of the people after that. I felt like it set back my work generally and delayed the project.

Microengagements

During the most difficult moments of the COVID-19 pandemic, microengagements were hard to come by. I instituted a daily thirty-minute meeting early in the pandemic for team members to review the past day and plan for the next. This coincided with the departure from the office of administrative and professional services staff. Conventional wisdom, which turned out to be right, suggested that office staff should work from home to slow down the spread of COVID.

From 4:30 p.m. to 5:00 p.m. Monday through Friday, we met as a team, usually six of us. A few months into this process, a manager who reported to me and attended the daily meetings said his team members always looked forward to end-of-day meetings because they provided access to a vice president. He said further those others in the company who were of similar age and experience had no such access, and having access really pumped up their engagement. Excellent! I hadn't planned it that way but was happy that was how it worked out.

Microrecognitions

Microrecognitions are qualitatively and quantitatively different from microengagements. Again, during the pandemic, at the point where the Delta variant was leading up to the Omicron variant, our recruiters were having difficulty in filling all the job requisitions submitted by the business. They worked round the clock, it seemed, to fill the entry-level roles. This was not easy since the pandemic required many recruiting-process changes. Our CEO became aware of trials afflicting recruiting and asked for a nice gift and card to be sent to the recruiters, thanking them, and recognizing them for their efforts. The microrecognition was relatively easy, was executed quickly, and had a positive impact.

I'm going to spend the rest of this chapter on microengagements and will return later to microrecognitions in chapter 8.

Happiness and Life Bests

I hope you know what it's like to be happy. Over your lifetime, there've been moments when all aspects of your existence came together at one time in harmony. Did you realize it when it happened? Did you think about the elements of the experience that created those positive feelings and caused them to wash over you in a wave? How long did the feelings of happiness and contentment persist? Research suggests that elements of happiness include the strength and size of your social network, physical health and environment, job opportunity, income (with many caveats), an overall sense of gratitude, and the ability to help others. Working in combination in our psyche, these elements of happiness create a state of being we crave.

I recall a moment in my late twenties when I felt this type of contentment. I was working for a financial services company in Cincinnati, Ohio. I enjoyed my assignment as a classroom trainer. I was part of the management team who had been charged with opening a new customer service center. I moved to Cincinnati to do this. The moment of my intense feeling of happiness occurred on a Saturday. That morning, I was out running errands. Later in the day, I had a date planned, a movie and dinner. I had a solid group of friends and some money in the bank. My clothes all fit and looked good on me. All was well with the world.

That wasn't the first or last moment when I felt that sense of contentment. Let's admit, though, that having everything come together at one time is an elusive prospect.

Striving for Career Bests

In my experience, some people don't quickly associate sensations of happiness with their current or past work or professional experiences. It's possible to do so, but additional elements need to come together. Above, I mentioned that current research suggests job opportunities are needed for happiness. If we go a little further into the research, we come upon the concept of a career best—not just opportunity but the reality from a job perspective. Different management models predict career bests as possibilities when there's an alignment of your skill set, your current job responsibilities, and your pay and rewards. It's still true, however, that social network, physical well-being, sense of gratitude, and ability to help others are important too.

Career best is a big thing, using the definition in the preface. Achieving a career best requires a huge amount of work and intentionality. It doesn't happen all at once but, rather, is produced gradually over time. Your manager, colleagues, and teammates also play a role in creating career bests—meaning they don't just happen by themselves. This is much more than micro*anything*; hence, I wanted to bring it up and now set it aside.

Understanding Microengagements

There are three sides at least to microengagement. We'll look at them in turn, after which we will think further about what leaders and managers can proactively do.

The first side of microengagement relates to a positive set of circumstances others create for you. For example, I was asked at one point in my career to participate in the benefits steering committee for a company. A group of business leaders met quarterly to review the state of benefits throughout the company and make decisions about what we'd do next to improve employee benefits. I served on the committee for ten years.

Roughly speaking, we met for eight to ten hours in total over a one-year period. If I use the standard 2,080 work hours per year, that's only one-half of 1 percent of standard time (does anyone work that anymore?). That number of hours per year is microengagement territory. Every time the committee met, I felt a burst of pride and happiness at having been asked to participate. The meetings and the process around them were microengagement moments brought about for me by a great manager who knew me well enough to appoint me to the committee.

The second side of microengagements relates to a positive set of circumstances you create for yourself. For example, I enjoy coaching early career professionals. Everything remains possible for them since they've been pursuing a career for less than five years when I start engaging with them. Whom I pick to coach is up to me. It's not strictly part of my job, but for me, the time I spend with these young people is microengaging. One young man I coached for about a year had reached a point where he was no longer satisfied with his job or the company. He was a member of two historically marginalized communities and needed a thinking partner to plan out his next career move. I was happy to help. Again, as with the first side of microengagements discussed above, the total amount of time spent was minimal.

The third side of microengagements relates to a positive set of circumstances you create for others. The early career coaching in the example above may qualify as two of the sides of microengagements, because both I and the person being coached were strongly engaged by the interactions. If we set aside any residual benefit that may accrue to you, this third side of microengagements is truly about others.

I like a strategy here that also creates a development opportunity for the individual. A manager on my team approached me about a microengagement he had in mind for a young person who reported to him. The ask was to send the employee to a project management class at the UW-Madison Center for Professional and Executive Development. "Yes, definitely," I said. "And are there more classes we should consider?" As in the other examples cited in this chapter, the amount of time spent in the class was a small percentage of the employee's total time, and an even smaller percentage of my time was required to consider the request and decide.

6

Understanding Appreciative Inquiry

In 2001, I was lucky enough to have a colleague, Pat, who was incredibly articulate and talented about interpersonal relationships and organizational dynamics. In my experience with Pat, he was able to cut through difficult situations to a core of positivity, something I couldn't do as readily and often neglected to try. I learned much from his techniques and still reflect on my learnings from Pat and his leadership and communication skills. In a one-on-one meeting with Pat, he brought up the concept of appreciative inquiry. It knocked me over. I hadn't heard about it before. Listening to Pat's explanation of AI prompted me to delve deeper.

Maybe you're already conversant. Let's review: appreciative inquiry (AI) was first written about by David Cooperrider and Suresh Srivastva in their 1987 article "Appreciative Inquiry in Organizational Life" published in *Research in Organizational Development and Change*. AI really hit the ground running, and in the thirty-five years since the article was published, it has found its way into the lexicon of organizational development professionals as a durable change and transformation methodology. Look up the article when you have time.

AI was the first meaningful managerial inquiry model to focus on what's working in an organization and what people care about as ways to drive positive transformation. The AI approach was the opposite of the then-predominant and still-popular deficiency model of inquiry, which presupposes the most effective way to create change is grounded in problem statements and hyperfocus on what's wrong and needs to be fixed. AI consists of five classic principles, one of which is the principle of positivity. This is what I'll focus on next.

On Positivity and Thoughtful Words

AI pushes us to a mindset of positive possibilities achieved through a questioning (or comment) strategy designed to surface what's right and good in the person or organization. Once we're at the point where words form and behavior is imminent, we can shape and target our microbehaviors to achieve maximum, long-lasting good.

As I said in chapter 1, a microbehavior is a small, short, detectable action. It can be spoken or visual. A microbehavior uses short phrases that convey meaning quickly and efficiently. The impact is generally immediate—and always positive when done right. We're continuing to honor this definition as we explore appreciative inquiry and generativity more fulsomely. Whether we're speaking of a microrecognition, microcompliment, or micromotivation, we're solidly in the realm of positive possibilities, as mentioned earlier.

In a panel interview via video recently, the panelists were posing questions to a candidate for a key HR business partner role. There were four of us on the panel. We needed to be thoughtful and appropriate. Looking at the screen, I contemplated the hiring manager, one of my colleagues. His name is Fez. I was suddenly very appreciative for everything he'd done to get to the point of hiring a new HRBP for a business group he'd been carefully tending to through a variety of big organizational changes.

This is what I said to the candidate: "Juanita, I want you to know that if the job works out, you'll be inheriting a group that has been well cared for. Fez has worked tirelessly to ensure that our new sales and marketing executives have received terrific HR consulting. Fez's long experience with the company gives him terrific perspective on how to advance our transformation. You'll enjoy Fez as your manager and colleague." Then I proceeded with my specific question for Juanita. It took almost no time to add the introductory comments, a microcompliment. It would've been a microrecognition too if other members of his team or his manager also had been present.

Let's turn to another example where an actual inquiry formed the basis of the microrecognition. I was in a room full of employees who were assembled to help with the design of a new manager development program. The employees had all been involved in a predecessor program based on some classic people manager principles that were no longer hitting the mark, in my opinion. These experienced employees gazed at me with skepticism. Those who know me in a professional setting may've expected me to launch into a critique of the current program while simultaneously advocating for a new one. Yup, once upon a time, that might've happened.

My Mentor and Me

MENTOR. These employees really believe in the current program. How're you going to handle this discussion? I worry you could set their teeth on edge if you come on too strong.

ARTELL. Yes. When I was hired at the company, an expectation was set to create a sustainable, repeatable manager curriculum. What I've used before would work fine.

MENTOR. But others in the company don't agree with the expectation. Why do you suppose that is?

ARTELL. Perhaps nobody talked to them about the expectation. That might not be far off the mark. But what I'm going to propose to them is better than what they have.

MENTOR. How do you know? What's your evidence?

ARTELL. Others have said this to me. They're thinking the other curriculum is not really making a difference in manager skills and in building relationships with employees.

MENTOR. Perhaps that's all true. But you lack empirical evidence. And you lack a strong understanding of the current approach. Wouldn't be a new thing for you to jump to the assumption that you're right and they're wrong.

ARTELL. What! Well, I mean, I guess. Yes, it's true that I resemble that comment. You know I can get passionate.

MENTOR. Yes, and I've seen you in those moments! How about this? Try meeting with them in only a discovery session. No advocacy.

ARTELL. But—

MENTOR. Hear me out. Use a technique that honors their position and all the work they've put into this over the years and try not to pick at what you're hearing. You need to build collaboration with them, not create opposition.

ARTELL. But—

MENTOR. Just try it. What harm could come? Then come back, and we'll talk more.

It won't surprise you to hear that my mentor was right. I didn't do exactly what he encouraged me to do, but it was close. When I got to the meeting, I'd already set the expectation that I just wanted to listen and understand. I'd asked if they could bring with them any materials they'd been using to teach. They were prepared to discuss the course in question, and I was fully prepared to absorb and ask questions.

We discussed the program for a couple of hours. They told me about the ups and downs of the company over their long tenure. I was able to use sincere microrecognitions and microcompliments along the way. You know what? I learned what I needed to about the supervisory program. Far more than that, I learned about them as individuals, including their struggles and successes. As the project progressed, they helped greatly with devising a new manager development program that sat comfortably next to the existing one.

Understanding Micromotivation

Motivation is both intrinsic and extrinsic. The former is motivation that originates from within, and the latter is motivation that originates from without. Motivation is about what you do, how hard you do it, and how persistent you are in doing it. Microrecognition and microcompliments fall into the category of extrinsic motivation, with the possibility of at least a partial migration to intrinsic motivation.

You and you alone are in control of whether you act on the microrecognitions and microcompliments to self-motivate. A manager who provides a micromotivation moment for you to capitalize on is trying to tap into your intrinsic needs in such a way that it prompts you to action. Examples of micromotivation behaviors or statements can include these:

- "I bet you'll enjoy the new assignment, even though you're only just hearing about it. I hope you go for it."
- "Don't worry about the little things you forgot to do; you remembered everything that was important."
- "You're invited to present the conclusion of the project to the CEO. Congratulations!"
- "I saw you in front of your team two days ago, and I have to say that I left inspired too!"

A note of caution: you could mess up someone's self-motivation, so be careful and intentional in your conversations. For example, saying to an employee who became recently very engaged in the work, "I'm glad you're demonstrating now that you care about the company instead of being a Donald Downer all the time!" is not the way to go. Even in typing out the example, I'm feeling less engaged in the work of writing this book! By using customized-to-the-employee microrecognitions and microcompliments, you'll become a more balanced person, be able to acknowledge the good others bring, and build truly durable relationships. Try it.

Microbehaviors and Coaching

I don't meet many people who are eager for developmental feedback. A few colleagues over the years have been exceptional in their desire to improve, but mostly, mediocrity thinking prevails. Feedback isn't always delivered in a way that promotes positive change. I don't love feedback, even the good stuff. Some feedback intended to move me in a better direction has occasionally caused me to move in the exact opposite direction.

There are lots of reasons why someone might not relish feedback, particularly of the developmental kind. One senior leader I worked with said to her boss that she wanted to call a halt to all developmental feedback for ninety days. I suspect she was suffering from feedback fatigue. But I also think she was suffering from poorly delivered feedback. Too direct? Probably. Too aggressive? Probably not, at least not at this company. Feedback should create opportunities, not destroy them.

One manager a few years ago delivered my annual performance review by starting out like this: "You're meeting expectations, but you've lost the confidence of the business leadership team."

Huh? I what? I thought. My response to this opening gambit was a combination of bewildered hurt, resistance, and complete surprise. Moreover, many of the people on the leadership team were longtime colleagues. We'd worked shoulder to shoulder together on many difficult projects. I could accept that the situation had deteriorated—I'm not a dummy. But had I lost the confidence of the entire team? Hardly. I eventually got to the bottom of what, who, and why, but it was a painful process, and I'm not sure I was better off at the end.

I don't believe my manager had any intent of injuring me with the feedback. It was his way, and I had a lot of respect for him. I just didn't respect the way the feedback was delivered. It lacked any kind of nuance in the sense of things that had been going well. Recall the previous chapter and the discussion about appreciative inquiry. He could've used better techniques to deliver the feedback. Here's my retrospective replay of the interaction with my manager. While the manager voice below is made up, my responses in this hypothetical situation are honest and reflect how I'd have answered at the time.

> MANAGER. We really appreciate everything you do for the company. Almost all your projects last year were heavy lifts, happening one right after the other. How're you feeling about your performance?

> ARTELL. Honestly, I don't feel I accomplished as much as I could. Having accountability over such a broad remit was challenging. Thanks for acknowledging that the lifts were heavy. I felt that way, and I'm chagrined I didn't really

discuss with you how I was faring. Or ask for your help.

MANAGER. I didn't offer help at the right moments. You were deeply involved in the HR technology upgrades, and I recognize you faced opposition. But you were still able to advance the project. I could've helped more. What would you say were the high points of the year? Not just the technology projects but all the high points.

Starting out in the fashion described above would've set the stage for the developmental feedback more effectively. It's not that I'd have received everything with a smile, wearing my heart on my sleeve. But the days, weeks, and months after the interaction wouldn't have been filled with such doubt and discouragement. You probably recall this line from a song in a famous Hollywood movie: "A spoonful of sugar helps the medicine go down." Amen.

Microcoaching and Developmental Feedback

I'm not infallible when it comes to delivering developmental feedback. I've stumbled into—OK, created—situations that were uncomfortable and off-putting for the employee. I recall an experience many years ago when I delivered some feedback to a teammate with whom I worked closely. She was the program manager for nonexempt base pay compensation at an oil company. I was the program manager for the exempt population.

We had compatible but different philosophies about compensation. She was much more experienced at the company than I was, but I was brash and full of myself. I said to her one day in a microcoaching moment something to the effect of "I know how to do this better than you." I didn't say it that way, but that was the drift.

My teammate reacted immediately and unhappily, not with anger but with genuine hurt and sadness. There were tears. I felt like a monster. Then I shed some tears. It wasn't a great situation for either of us. Not knowing what else to say or do, I left her office, resolved not to do that again and to think more carefully in advance of the interaction.

What happened next time? The same thing. Yikes. Still a monster. Then I went to talk to our manager and got some practical advice about how not to make people cry when delivering feedback. Useful stuff that was! Ultimately, the relationship was repaired, and I learned how to use my words better and not act like a bull in a china shop. (It's possible she used that metaphor about me.)

What I had to say to my teammate was in the vein of microcoaching. All I really wanted to do was to coach her on some of the nuances of compensating the research staff, in the hope the information could be useful for the work she did with lab technicians, who were the backbone of the facility. Simply put, this was the coaching I had in mind: "Let's talk before we make the final recommendations about pay increases for technicians and researchers who work closely together. I think we could really help managers to better focus on all three elements of the environment: performance, context, and relationships."

Was that so hard to say? Why did I fumble it so badly? I think the explanation is within the requirement to remove yourself from the equation. In other words, don't deliver microcoaching with a mindset of *I know how to do this better than you*. Rather, deliver it with only the good of the other person in mind. Microcoaching with yourself at the center will always come across with a holier-than-thou attitude. Zero in instead on how to help the individual take the next step toward improved performance without your ego as part of the delivery mechanism.

Brag, Worry, Wonder, Bet and Microcoaching Opportunities

In Steve King's book *Brag, Worry, Wonder, Bet: A Manager's Guide to Delivering Feedback (BWWB)*, readers learn about a methodology that can be used to move employees along the performance spectrum, always improving. To really get the feel of BWWB, you should read the book. It's short and sweet and to the point. I first heard about BWWB when I worked for Steve in the late 1990s. We worked for the same consultancy, and he'd been charged with helping managers to deliver feedback without injuring the manager-employee relationship.

I've sometimes heard leaders say, across multiple different companies, that feedback is a gift. Maybe. When I have been gifted with feedback, I've more than once thought it would be nice to return it for a nice sweater! In the case of the organization that Steve and I worked for, they needed a more digestible approach to delivering feedback, versus "Here's the gift you didn't ask for" delivered in a way that was painful. The BWWB model was it:

- *Brag* is exactly what it sounds like. For example, "When I think about you, Ellen, I want to brag about your ability to simplify complex topics into actionable steps."

- *Worry* is also exactly what it sounds like. For example, "When I think about you, Ellen, I tend to worry that you're going too fast for others to keep up with you."
- *Wonder* is a bit more nuanced. It's characterized by the classic definition but sits in a feedback frame where you really don't know the answer. For example, "When I think about you, Ellen, I wonder whether you'll be able to improve your objectivity and use data effectively."
- *Bet* too has a nuance, again in the sense that it sits in a feedback frame but including an intuitive leap. For example, "When I think of you, Ellen, I bet you'll be able to overcome this current challenge and grow your career over the next five years."

I've now used BWWB in four different companies since Steve first inducted me into this methodology. In all circumstances, the BWWB framework has been a godsend. It possesses the key characteristics of simplicity, brevity, and accuracy. Little is left to the imagination when discussions are handled properly. It's important to customize what you're going to say to the person in these microcoaching moments. Let's conclude our microcoaching chapter by considering some negative examples and their positive counterparts of microcoaching:

Examples of Microcoaching Using BWWB

	Negative Microcoaching	Positive Microcoaching
Brag	• "Keep up the great work on Acme, but let's try not to tick off the boss the next time you need something." • "Thanks for handling Ted's issue. I'm sure he liked your high-intensity approach to feedback." • "You and Tomasz sure made an impression on the oversight committee. They were so dazed at the end."	• "Great work on the Acme project. You care about your team, and it shows when you advocate for resources." • "Ted appreciates the time you spent with him. You were direct but fair. I think he'll improve." • "You and Tomasz thoroughly presented risks at the oversight committee. They have all they need to make the decision."
Worry	• "Devon, we need to talk. I'm pretty sure you're going to miss the product launch deadline. Better get moving." • Matt, the vendor seems to really be making a mess of things. Have you been managing them closely?"	• "Hi, Devon! Got a minute? I'm a little worried about the timeline for the product launch. What are your thoughts?" • "I'm a little worried, Matt, about the performance system. How confident are you about the vendor's response?"

		""Morgan, you know that everyone has family stuff to deal with. Why haven't I heard from you? There's really no excuse."	• "Morgan, it's great to see you! I've been worried about your family situation. What can we do to ease your stress?"
Wonder	•	"Leon, are you as discouraged as I am about the acquisition? I wonder when we'll get the bad news. What will you do?" • "You make me wonder all the time about the unstable future of this technology. How will we ever pay for the development?" • "Don't you wonder when the CEO will call in rich and leave us all hanging? We're the ones who will be screwed on this process. She won't care."	• "Leon, are you wondering about the same thing I am? Sure feels like things could go either way with the acquisition. Thoughts?" • "You make me wonder all the time about the future of this technology. Feels like opportunity is in front of us!" • "Don't you wonder sometimes how long our CEO will stay around? I know I do. She has a lot to think about, and you and I should prepare for change."

| **Bet** | • "So many terrible things could happen with the campaign. I don't see us succeeding. Your team's odds to win are poor." | • "So many options for the new advertising campaign. I'm betting we'll figure it out soon. Has your team weighed in?" |
| | • "You think we should bet a dinner at Mr. B's over the public offering? I'm betting they'll take us all down to the wire in suspense." | • "You think we should bet a dinner at Mr. B's over this public offering? I'm betting they'll find a way to get financing lined up." |

Preparing ahead of time for microcoaching moments, especially when the individual might not initially agree, is critical to maintaining motivation and forward progress. If you have a doubt about how the feedback and coaching could be received, practice with a peer or your manager. Recovering from a poor microcoaching moment takes a lot of time, which you probably don't have in abundance.

7

Microbehaviors and Meetings

Recently, I was on the phone with my dentist's office, trying to schedule an appointment to have an implant seated. I'd called them because almost double the time I'd been promised had passed, and still no implant. The administrative assistant's name was Stephanie, and we'd met several times before. She chided me, saying she had left a voice mail for me two weeks previous but hadn't heard back. I protested mildly and told her I always check voice mail at the end of a day because I'm usually tied up in meetings otherwise.

Again, Stephanie chided me and said that surely I had time between meetings to listen to voice mail. After a long, pregnant pause, I told her that almost my entire work life consisted of meetings, and some days there was just no daylight between meetings to do as she'd coached me. Stephanie was skeptical, and we turned back to trying to schedule the appointment. We landed on 7:15 a.m.

What's the problem with the story above? The part about my being in meetings almost all day long is true. I'm embarrassed to admit that. How did I arrive at a place where my time is no longer strictly my own? In theory, I should be able to exercise a lot of control over my calendar. However, calendar management, for me, has become more like playing a game of Tetris than exercising real control.

My Mentor and Me

ARTELL. We aren't having much success in getting the consulting and outsourcing business leaders together for the change management workshop they agreed to. Their calendars are impossible. The next available time is eight weeks out.

MENTOR. That's too long to wait. They need help coalescing as a team, and this change management workshop is designed for that purpose. We've engaged an outside consultant, Jeff, and he's tough to get.

ARTELL. No argument from me. How do you want me to handle it? I can get all the executive assistants together to discuss.

MENTOR. Yes, do that. And I'm going to discuss in the staff meeting tomorrow. If they can't control their calendars, then who can?

ARTELL. It's not that you are wrong; it's just that you're not 100 percent right. I will encourage everyone to lean into the calendars.

My mentor's final comment brought me up short. It's true: If the senior business leaders of the company can't control their calendars and accommodate important stuff, then who can? I learned early in my career that I shouldn't ask senior leaders to change their calendars in favor of mine. They had important things to do, and my small doings could wait. I've applied this logic to scheduling for nearly forty years. Some days it's painful—worse than going to the dentist!

Meetings are like the weather. Everyone complains, but nobody does anything about them. They're a necessary organizational construct. They serve a purpose, but my belief is that calling a meeting should be more of a final option, not the first option. How do I know this has gotten out of hand? Because about 20 percent of the meetings I'm invited to are preparation meetings for the meeting. Jiminy Christmas! Almost any communication and interaction vehicle would be better versus meetings to plan for meetings. The fact they exist is due partly to a lack of creativity but also to a lack of effective meeting management generally. I'm as guilty as the next person.

Before I move on to a discussion of microbehaviors and meetings, I want to state that there are some best practices for calendar management. Here are a few you may consider:

- **Standing meetings:** If you need a standing meeting—daily, weekly, monthly, or quarterly—pick the longest period between meetings you can safely imagine. You can always add in more time. Canceling meetings at the last minute tends to irritate people.
- **Calendar delegation:** While this seems like a good idea, it also presents problems. Once you delegate all or part of your calendar, you can assume that all available time will get used up. Keep your own calendar for as long as you can, and only delegate selectively.

- **Phantom meetings:** This is an old but effective trick. Block phantom meeting time on your calendar to enable yourself to get stuff done. For many years, my assistant Kathy blocked several hours of time weekly under the name of my former graduate school professors. Most people never figured it out. Whenever I saw one of their names, I knew I could use that time.
- **The rule of thirty:** Over my career, I've mostly seen meetings follow the rule of thirty, meaning thirty-minute meetings or multiples thereof. I'm sure you've heard that meetings take up the time allotted, even if you could've accomplished what's needed in less time. Scheduling a twenty-minute or ten-minute meeting is fair game. It sets expectations. Or if you need a seventy-five-minute meeting, don't book it for ninety minutes under the notion that you must follow the rule of thirty.

Microbehaviors in Meetings and Emotional Intelligence

Microbehaviors in a meeting, whether in person, hybrid, or remote, can dramatically affect the outcome of the meeting. I'm not talking about all the premeeting activities, such as who's invited and the content, agenda, or location. Rather, I'm referring to what's said in the meeting, including tone, pace, word choice, comment length, questions posed, and facial expressions. Nearly all microbehaviors in a meeting will convey meaning of some kind. Emotion comes with meaning, whether contentment, happiness, sadness, frustration, confusion, anger, or another emotion. Because of this daisy chain that commences with a microbehavior and ends with emotion and probably action, it's important to self-regulate throughout.

Self-regulation is one of Dan Goleman's five elements of emotional intelligence, which is the set of qualities and behaviors that allow a mature, thinking person to navigate human interactions in confident and appropriate ways. The other four are self-awareness, motivation, empathy, and social skills. You can read all about Goleman's model in his book *Emotional Intelligence: Why It Can Matter More Than IQ* (2005). There are other emotional intelligence models, of course. I recommend you look at *The Handbook of Emotional Intelligence: Theory, Development, Assessment, and Application at Home, School, and in the Workplace* (2000) by Reuven Bar-On, James D. A. Parker, et al. A quick online search will reveal another dozen research-oriented publications and websites where you can read even more on the EI topic. All these models are legitimate points of reference and will help guide you through conversations in which you're working to demonstrate emotional intelligence.

What specifically can be done before a meeting starts to pave the way to positive microbehaviors during the meeting? I noted above the obvious things that should be done prior to a meeting. Don't forget those. I recall a meeting I scheduled years ago to which I invited people whom I didn't know but who were important to the project I was leading. I'd prepared a simple agenda, and I started the meeting by handing it out. There was a brief silence, and the most senior person in the room, the director of pension services, looked at my manager and said, "Where did you get this guy from? I can't remember the last time anyone had prepared an agenda, and I must say, it's refreshing." The agenda was something small that helped to pave the way for a better meeting.

But that's not all. Other things you can do to ensure a meeting has a plentiful sufficiency of positive microbehaviors include these:

1. Send a note to meeting participants, asking if there are any topics they want to cover that aren't already on the agenda.
2. Ask whether anyone has any special situations that might prevent him or her from coming to the meeting.
3. Determine whether any invitees will be joining from remote locations, and ensure the technology is available in the room and in good working condition.
4. Think about whether the meeting length or time of day suggests that bottles of water or snacks should be provided and tell the invitees.
5. Consider the demographics of those invited to the meeting. Are there members of nondominant cultures? Are there potential language-comprehension challenges?

There are many other possibilities you could run through to help prepare for the meeting. One last thing I will mention is this: in a situation where conflict on some level is likely, I practice comments I could make to defuse the situation quickly. More than once, I've been grateful to have a few words on my lips ready to verbalize as needed.

Positive Microbehaviors in Meetings

Let's consider examples of positive microbehaviors you can rely upon to help meetings proceed and conclude productively. I'm approaching this from the four perspectives: facial expression, voice tone and pace, word choice, and demonstrated emotion. It's important to state that there are also cultural and social nuances you need to understand to convey what you intend. Plus, keep in mind that too much of any positive behavior will lead those observing you to wonder if you're being insincere or manipulative.

Facial Expressions and Head Movements	• Give a sincere, fluid smile, meaning not a frozen smile but one that plays across your face with genuine congeniality. • Nod with the culturally appropriate head bob, showing continued interest in what the person is saying. • Display an expectant look of curiosity characterized by slightly raised eyebrows and a mouth turned up at its edges.
Voice Tone and Pace	• Maintain even modulation that neither rises nor falls too quickly, wherein intonation is reflective of a sociable state of mind. • Deliver comments like those you'd use when meeting someone new, when a good first impression is important. • Accentuate slightly the positive words in your comments—for example, "This will be a huge success!"
Word Choice	• Select positive words as you speak, such as *good, better, best, amazing, great, considerable, desirable, dependable,* and so on. • Refrain from using negative words in reverse. For example, "I think we'll make excellent progress" is better than "I'm sure we'll make not inconsiderable progress."

Demonstrated Emotions	• Verbalize using facial expressions and tones that indicate you're in the right place at the right time, with no regrets.
	• Gravitate to positive emotions that demonstrate a belief that the team and individuals can solve problems.
	• Declare which emotion you're feeling, positive or negative, and why to promote understanding and bypass doubt.
	• Impute positive feelings and intent to all present; showing anger, even if nonspecific, will worry everyone present.

Successful Positive Microbehaviors for Meetings

When you're in doubt about how best to proceed in a meeting, especially if you feel things are going poorly, there are a few microbehaviors you can use to get things on track. While all behaviors, if overused, can be misunderstood, selective use of these will make you feel more at ease in tough situations.

- Say in a neutral tone with a slight smile, "Let's back up a bit and summarize where we are. Let me try, and please correct me!"
- Say in an upbeat and pleasant tone with eyebrows raised a bit, "We're all working hard to get through the issues in front of us, and I know we'll succeed. I could use a Diet Coke. How about you? Reconvene in ten."
- Say with a slight accentuation on key words and a broad smile, "I need to say that I'm *thoroughly* impressed with our discussion. We're going to solve this problem for sure."
- Say in a deadpan manner with a curious expression, "I bet we'll be able to have this kind of fun every time we meet. Let's wrap things for today and sleep on it."

Many other microbehaviors could work for you, and I'd encourage you to think about organization culture references that might help. In my experience, those kinds of references can be very effective. For example, before I joined my current company as a regular employee, I was a consultant for a year. At first, I was navigating the culture with one eye closed. I'd not seen enough to get my feet under me, and I had foot-in-mouth disease.

After a particularly tough meeting, when my microbehaviors were conveying a combination of skepticism and frustration,

I received a phone call from one of the meeting participants. Henry said to me that I was losing the confidence of members of the project team because I was being too specific and too harsh. Yikes! That's the last thing a consultant wants to hear.

"Artell, you aren't exhibiting sufficient trust in managing your relationships on this project. When direction is given and committed to, trust the work will get done." Henry further said that it was expected there would be an inspection routine.

I was grateful for his feedback, and it resonated with me. Constantly harping on project deliverables when they were not yet due and when there were no obvious problems was disrespectful. I apologized in the next meeting, and we went on in a much more congenial fashion.

One way I've been able to infuse more trust in my work is by delegating decision-making authority to others. When I traveled to India over a period of fifteen years or so, the trips lasted more than one week—four to five business days, plus the weekend on each side. The CEO I supported, correctly, wanted to have his HR leader available for whatever came up. Once or twice, he searched for me and found an empty desk—not a good look for a chief human resources officer! Instead of leaving things to chance, I asked one of my three direct reports to sit at my desk when I was on one of those long trips. I promised each of the three excellent professionals I asked to sit in for me, "I will support any decision you make. No questions asked." I was grateful to have them on the team.

Communication and Change Management

I'm not a geneticist or anything like it, but I do read, and I learned something new just recently: our DNA changes as much as 20 percent over a period of ten to sixteen years. The changes we all experience over time are called DNA methylation. The process of methylation impacts how genes are used and can make us susceptible to certain diseases. Our propensity to experience methylation can be passed on from generation to generation. Literally, change is built into our DNA. We may not be fully aware of it, but it impacts us nonetheless. If you want to know more about methylation, just connect with Uncle Google.

I'm bringing up methylation because of the number of people who have said to me over the years that they don't want to change and don't like change. These statements about not changing or liking change are ironic, considering the above information. Interestingly, many follow up their antichange comment with something like "But I'm flexible." Huh? Are people confusing change as being something much more momentous that it really is? Flexibility is but one manifestation of our ability to change. I think most of us demonstrate some level of flexibility every day in some way.

Since March 2020, we've all be experiencing changes in our lives because of the COVID-19 pandemic. You may say that any changes related to the pandemic were thrust upon us, so we had no choice but to change. That's not true, though. We still had many choices, and I know many people who stubbornly maintained their positions throughout the pandemic, with no attempt to change or to exhibit flexibility. So be it. Forcing change, even smart change, usually doesn't work.

People will get their dander up over the craziest things. For example, "What! You don't offer fried meat loaf on your menu anymore? Then I won't be eating here anymore!" The proverbial baby getting thrown out with the bathwater. Or "We've been doing it this way for years. Why mess with success?" Oh, we've reached perfection. How great! Yes, I say this with tongue firmly in cheek. These reactions aren't productive but are all too common. Collective change fatigue, combined with stubbornness and a critical lack of flexibility, makes for glacial change, if any change at all.

I'm not a proponent of change for change's sake. When in brainstorming meetings on improving productivity, more than once, I have heard this phrase: "We just need to change it up and see what happens." Um, no. Let's not do that. Messing with the minds of employees is never a good idea. If you have a reason for change and a better way, state the information clearly, or nobody follows.

When I was in graduate school, I had a terrific communications professor who taught a class for all MPA, MBA, MOB, and MAcc students. I was sloppy in my writing at that point. It was easy for me to wander away from a central thesis, and the professor repeatedly emphasized that business leaders need information in digestible forms—the shorter the better. A common triplet he repeated many times to us was the following:

- Tell them what you're going to tell them.
- Tell them what you need to tell them.
- Tell them what you told them.

I took this to heart, and over the years, I have frequently used these phrases. Interestingly, the first reference to this sage counsel is traced to a lay clergyman in England who described this same process when he prepared his Sunday sermons.[5] That's all about change too but on a more basic core level! The simplicity of it is appealing and points to the center of any change management effort: repeated and repeatable communications.

You know the value of clear communications within your organization. A nicely written, pithy email can go a long

---

[5] "Three Parts of a Sermon," *Hartlepool Northern Daily Mail*, August 13, 1908, 3.

way toward helping employees get it. The same goes for a thoughtful script for a town hall session or video shoot. Any preplanned or prerecorded message can benefit from a detailed examination of everything from the use of unhelpful multisyllable words to grammar and punctuation. I've always thought that a natural writing style that mimics the spoken word has the best chance of hitting the mark.

A senior communications consultant who was attached to a large business transformation project interviewed me one cold afternoon in a suburb of Chicago. He was meeting with all the leaders attached to the project to review the communications plan he'd put together after a stakeholder analysis. Along the way, he said to me something like this: "Look, you're a mature, seasoned business leader, and you need to simplify what you're saying about this project."

I stared at him for a long moment before I said, "I'm one of the most junior leaders on this project, and I'm not sure how much simpler I can make it. Everyone else has been there and done that." The consultant then walked me through in more detail what he meant, and he had me dead to rights. I was being overly complex in my explanations, and my communication was confusing the teams I was attached to. Also, I wasn't taking obvious moments to advocate properly for the changes at hand.

Next, we'll look at some micro–change management behaviors you can use at almost any time that will improve your communications generally. My intent here is not to dumb things down. Rather, my intent is to help you make more targeted comments about what's important, using straightforward language. Here's what I mean:

Not This	Instead, This
"I support the reengineering proposal that was put forth by the continuous improvement team. It will enable a major productivity improvement over the next four quarters."	"I support the CI team's plan. We'll see solid improvement over the next year."
"Betty, you seem to be struggling in accomplishing almost all your daily tasks. I am considering whether we should put you on a personal improvement plan."	"Betty, it seems like daily tasks are a struggle for you. I'm thinking we should collaborate on a plan to help you get tasks done."
"We won't be able to request any further pricing increases from our tier-one clients. They will direct us back to section fourteen of the contract and say we're in breach."	"Price increases won't fly with our largest clients. They will read the contract and say we aren't following it."
"Our CEO, Janice, has been preparing us for major changes in our product offerings for at least the last three years. We should have listened more carefully along the way since now we're struggling to achieve our revenue targets. It's not too late, but we need to go much faster."	"Janice was right. She's been telling us for years, but we weren't paying attention. We slid into a ditch and need to get out. It's not too late, but we must hurry."

"Our new headquarters building is almost complete. We now need to create a plan to announce what will be different when we move. For example, the overall space per employee is twenty-five percent less than this building, which is why we need to get people ready for a cube versus a private office environment. You should make yourselves available to speak to any employee who is struggling with this change."	"The new building has twenty-five percent less space. Expect fewer private offices and more cubes. Some people won't adapt well, and we need to communicate the plan soon. I'm happy to talk to anyone who is dragging his or her feet."

Everything on the left above is standard corporate speech. The message is conveyed but is stilted. I took the examples from things I've said and written over the years. Unfortunately, I had a lot to choose from! On the right are simplified versions that convey the same messages but more simply and quickly. "Point of order," you might say. "Sometimes the formality is required!" Well, yes, that's true. But unlike with formal reports, government filings, and legal actions, there are many times when formality is not needed. Chase those down and make the message simple.

There are rarely moments when change management is perfectly received. Don't wait for the stars, galaxies, and alternate universes to align. If you see a reasonable opening to support change, whatever the stated reason is to be together, you should seize the moment. You can sometimes make a great impression on others with a well-timed, well-tuned non sequitur.

The Gunning Fog Index

The Gunning Fog Index (GFI) is a great way to see how well you're doing on simplifying your communication, all in the spirit of better understandability and change management outcomes. Remember the professor I mentioned early in this chapter? Well, the GFI was a favorite tool of his. Essentially, the index allows you to get a handle on the education level you're writing at.

The calculation is relatively simple to do and even simpler if you Google "Gunning fog calculator" and just plug in what you've written. The calculator will spit out the education level of your written word. The recommendation is that writing should not be greater than twelfth grade and should hover around eighth grade to be effective. I've heard that many newspapers write at around the fourth- or fifth-grade level. This chapter on microbehaviors and change management, ironically, scores at the tenth-grade level. The preface scores at ninth grade, and chapter 6, which is about the midpoint of the book, scores at eighth grade.

8

Microbehaviors and Personality

I've saved the subject of personality for last. Not because I think it's the most or least important but because it's foundational for behavioral calibration. Understanding your personality style and what comes naturally to you is a key component in your quest for self-awareness and self-regulation. Call out to Goleman's emotional intelligence model!

I think my own personality traits are endlessly interesting, at least to me. Not everyone feels as positively about my personality as I do, since I've occasionally been coached to adjust certain traits dynamically. It's highly likely that people around you are sometimes hoping you will also adjust your personality traits from time to time. Why do we behave automatically when it comes to certain situations, but in other situations, we need to work much harder to demonstrate appropriate behaviors?

Doing what comes naturally is easy. We encounter people at work or home or in our communities, and our natures are manifested through our behaviors. Have you ever felt yourself being guarded? Have you been in situations where you weren't really being yourself or the full, complete you? Why do we do that? Are we concerned that people won't like who we are? Or is it that we're not ready to trust the other person fully? Maybe it's a little of everything. In my case, it's because I worry I may come on too strong. One manager I had said this to me: "Artell, you have a deplorable excess of personality." I took it as a compliment, but I know he said it as a way for me to understand the fact that less of me was more in some cases.

Discovering Your Basic Behaviors

In chapter 2, I listed a few popular and frequently used personality assessments. Among the assessments I've personally used on a regular basis are the Myers-Briggs Type Indicator (MBTI); DiSC; StrengthsFinder; Minnesota Multiphasic Personality Inventory (MMPI); Motives, Values, Preferences Inventory (MVPI); and Hogan Personality Inventory (HPI). No matter which personality assessment I've used over the years, I've been identified as possessing the same traits overall. My MBTI type is ENTJ. When I teach the MBTI in basic entry-level manager classes, I introduce myself as a recovering ENTJ. Why? Because I want to acknowledge clearly that being only or all one thing does not create great experiences for those around me.

Much research has been done on personality traits and the differentiation of traits. The five groupings of personality traits are openness, conscientiousness, extraversion, agreeableness, and neuroticism. A little online searching will land you at many descriptions of the Big Five, and you can take as many assessments as you wish. The Open-Source

Psychometrics Project is a good place to start, and you could branch out from there. Here are definitions of the Big Five personality traits (or groupings) commonly agreed upon by psychologists,[6] expressed in my own words:

---

[6] The theory of the existence of five basic personality traits was developed in 1949 by D. W. Fiske and later expanded upon by other researchers, including Warren T. Norman, Lewis R. Goldberg, Robert McCrae, Paul Costa, and others.

Trait	Common Characteristics
Openness	Characterized by an eagerness to learn, insightful observations, an active imagination, and broad interests.
Conscientiousness	Characterized by high self-regulation, a propensity to set and achieve goals, a desire for order, and detail-orientation.
Extraversion (Extroversion)	Characterized by a high need to be in the company of others, a propensity for emotional expressiveness, and loquaciousness.
Agreeableness	Characterized by a desire to help others, be trusting, and demonstrate empathy and cooperativeness.
Neuroticism	Characterized by a bias to overidentify perceived threats in daily life, frequent sadness and moodiness, and an inability to cope with stress and anxiety.

I'd like to remind you here that there are no right or correct personality styles. The demonstration of personality-driven behaviors derives from genetics, environment, and context. Different situations call for different behaviors. If you've a propensity for any of the above traits, then the descriptive words speak for themselves. But if you find yourself exhibiting a multiplicity of behaviors across all these traits, that reality for you is no less valid than the reality of someone who falls squarely into only one of the Big Five.

For example, being goal-oriented is frequently seen as a laudable trait in organizational settings. But I know many people—friends, family, colleagues—who don't think much about goals and have little use for them. They believe that doing one's best while enjoying life from one moment to the next is sufficient. They do not need SMART (specific, measurable, achievable, relevant, time-bound) goals to feel productive and complete.

Identifying Desired Personality-Driven Microbehaviors in Context

You've probably noticed that I haven't yet listed out many microbehaviors pertinent to personality traits. The reason? The behaviors needed in common organizational leadership situations should be divorced from the natural behavior of the manager or leader. Well, not entirely divorced, but individual managers need to model behaviors that may or may not be based on their natural inclinations. In the section heading, I used the word *context*. Here are common contexts that require certain types of productive behaviors:

1. Sourcing and recruiting candidates
2. Onboarding and orienting new employees

3. Managing the performance of employees
4. Coaching and developing employees
5. Communicating to employees
6. Recognizing and rewarding employees

These contexts are all part of the employee life cycle. Similar activities can be described in both client and customer settings. I've left out exiting employees, since these moments are generally governed by forces other than the personality traits of managers. Everything else is about adapting your behavior as needed for the context. I set out below a few microbehaviors organized by the six talent life-cycle events.

Sourcing and Recruiting	• "You've had some great experiences during your career. Say more about what you hope to do next." • "What're the kinds of projects you enjoy the most? Your previous work suggests you're very flexible." • "I feel like we're hitting it off well, and I'm learning a lot about your professional interests. Please ask me anything you want about why I've stayed here." • "Looking from the outside, it might be hard to see how the company cares for its employees. What do you expect to see to demonstrate that we really do care?"
Onboarding and Orienting	• "There's much to learn as you come on board. We don't want to overwhelm you. What's your preferred way to take in and retain new information?" • "So glad you decided to join us! Our culture is unique, and I thought I'd spend a few minutes to describe how I experience it. Please ask any questions!" • "We wanted to provide structure to your orientation. Here's your agenda for the next sixty days." • "How's your family doing with the move? I'm familiar with that kind of stress. What can we do to help?"

Managing Performance	• "Your accomplishments last year are many, and the company is grateful. Let's talk about this year's goals. What do you have in mind?" • "I know I'm being very direct with you, and I see that you're uncomfortable. We should take a break and go for a walk." • "Things are moving so fast! You're critical to our success. I'm thinking we should meet more regularly. What would make sense?"
Coaching and Developing	• "We need an out-of-box idea to solve this problem. You're so creative. I haven't always appreciated that in you. Don't hold back! Let's consider all possibilities." • "Let's find a quiet place for a short conversation. I've seen you in action with our executives before. Something was different today. Thoughts?" • "The time has arrived! You worked so hard on your development plan. Let's schedule out the fastest way to get you that management certificate."
Communicating	• "We must maintain close contact since the team is depending on us. There are many details in our communications. What works best for you?" • "I want to ensure we continue to stay aligned. Even if we disagree sometimes, I know our relationship will get stronger as we weather this together."

	• "Every day we should connect with our teammates. Some want texts, others want emails, and still others need the personal touch of in-person regroups."
Recognizing and Rewarding	• "Hi, Jorge. Let's talk a bit about Piotr's ten-year celebration. I know he doesn't love big events. Let's throw the rule book out and plan something small." • "Hello, everyone. Before we start our regular meeting, I want to pause to recognize two members of our team who have done some amazing things recently." • "Tricia, you haven't been on vacation for almost a year. We appreciate all you do, especially your willingness to pitch in anywhere. We want to send you and your two children to Disney for a week. Congratulations!"

My Mentor and Me

ARTELL. I know that you aren't in love with personality assessments. Of course, your being an INTJ goes well with that opinion!

MENTOR. You know I don't speak MBTI. All those letters. That's your department. I think too much focus on personality could cause people to miss the point.

ARTELL. Which is? I mean, what's the point we could be missing? I agree that too much focus on personality gives people a false sense that personality-driven behaviors are the right ones.

MENTOR. Exactly my point. The behaviors leaders need to exhibit should arise from the context, from the situation. The reflective mind needs to be fully engaged. Automatic mind behavior, which frequently erupts from personality, can easily miss the mark.

ARTELL. I know you're right. Achieving self-awareness, and then self-regulation, takes more input than just a personality assessment. What're you thinking about?

MENTOR. Some of the best observations come from 360 feedback. I don't mean the ordinary feedback you can get via an annual performance review but assessments that are a combination of self-evaluation and the evaluations of others.

ARTELL. You mean assessments like the one used by the Center for Creative Leadership or Human Synergistics or perhaps the Hogan?

MENTOR. Yes, they're a little complicated but worth it. All these 360 assessments describe behavior that leaders need to model. You can't get there with personality only.

The Dangers of Oversharing

I've been thinking about the intersection of microbehaviors, specifically your microbehaviors and the microbehaviors of those around you, and what happens when everything becomes confusing and perhaps overwhelming. You know what I mean—those moments when everything you thought you knew becomes irrelevant in the face of something completely new that you must now deal with. In my experience, those moments are produced when honesty, trust, and familiarity align in a perfect storm of candor and openness. We all know that storms can be raucous affairs in which things that are solid and steady can be uprooted and flung about with reckless abandon.

Building relationships with your employees can have the unintentional consequence of putting you in a situation where you know more than is healthy to know about an individual. The work environment is one that needs curation, meaning there are conversations that shouldn't take place or should be banked and cooled when they arise. If the action of getting to know someone and building trust causes oversharing, you could have more on your hands than you would strictly want. Let's walk down this road together and see what we find.

In a casual conversation with an employee, you may hear something personal; for example, you could become privy to information about a marital problem, difficulty with children, or even a dangerous addiction of some kind. You could also hear information about financial troubles, medical conditions, or legal problems. All of these are potentially serious situations that require professional help—the kind of help you're not required to provide, however deeply attached you may be to the employee with whom you're having the discussion.

Sometimes the pressure of a difficult situation pushes an employee to say more than he or she intends or should. The employee may be projecting too much onto the relationship and making up a story about how it makes sense to share with you details of his or her personal situations. I've been in this position before, and it's distinctly uncomfortable.

An employee came to me once to discuss a divorce situation. The divorce was messy and had child custody components too. The employee wanted my advice on what to do next and how to go about winning the custody case. As much as I cared about the employee and counted the person as a friend—we had been to each other's home—there was no way I could or would opine on a divorce or child custody suit. All I could do was refer the person to the company's employee assistance program (EAP) for help and to human resources for details on any FMLA possibilities. However, in this situation, I did entertain questions and requests about current workload and assignments. That was something I could control and perhaps provide relief on, if needed.

I recognize there's a paradox here since I've been part of the human resources department at every company for which I've worked. But I've never been an expert on all facets of all HR programs and benefit plans. I have capable colleagues who know more than I do, and I'm not concerned about admitting that there are many HR things on which I'm not an authority.

While you shouldn't indulge employee questions on topics about which you know little or nothing, you should continue to create a safe environment in which all employees can function in a healthy way. Consider rereading chapters 5 and 6 for pointers on creating and maintaining the right environment. As a manager, your accountability ends at the point where the private life of the employee begins. I try not to ask many questions about a person's private life unless he or she has given me the signal that it's OK to do so. On the other hand, I do invite questions about my personal life by describing what goes on outside the four walls of the company.

When I'm in the midst of sharing my personal details, I try to stick on the sunny side to help others view me in a more human and humane way. In some cases, my propensity to divulge prompts others to divulge too. Never do I press for more than what's offered, nor do I play a one-up game in which I offer something even more personal or impactful than what the other person has revealed. When in doubt about what to say or do, go talk to your helpful, friendly HR partner.

Conclusion

As business leaders, it's our duty to effectively manage our microbehaviors in the workplace. Opportunities to do so present themselves every day. While we all sometimes stray into the negative, letting our emotions get the best of us, which in turn leads us to say or do something without giving it enough thought, that should be the exception rather than the rule.

Trust me. I speak from personal experience. I'm self-aware about my own microbehaviors, but I still struggle to keep myself in check, since I can get passionate and emotional about my favorite topics, such as microbehaviors. The trick is to keep the focus on the needs of employees. When I do that, I know I'll make a positive impact. I'm not always successful in my efforts, but I'm steadily improving.

If you make the effort, you can effectively manage your microbehaviors as a business leader, setting an example for your team to follow. Consciously set a goal to begin any interactions with other people based on the human side of the equation. In other words, make it clear that you care about the other members of your team before getting down to handling whatever task is at hand. Work through challenging situations with an appreciative inquiry style that's conducive to conflict-free management when the going gets tough.

You are in the driver's seat in terms of how microbehaviors impact your business. You've already taken the first big step forward in effectively managing your microbehaviors simply by reading this book and becoming aware of how important it is to sweat the small stuff. Little things, such as how you word an email or how you address a challenging issue with the team, make all the difference between running a successful, thriving business and running one that limps along almost in spite of itself. You now have the tools to move forward to take the next step to enact the best microbehavioral management practices, leading your company down the path to stellar success.

AFTERWORD

I have long thought that management development—or leadership development, if you prefer—is rarely about a massive overhaul of a manager's approach to managing. Rather, key improvements come from a collection of small behavioral adjustments akin to the small adjustments jazz trumpeters make to improve their tone or timing.

I found Artell quite candid in this book about his own shortcomings when it comes to the right kinds of microbehaviors. I've known him for a long while, and I can assure you his positive impact far outweighs any negative. But that candid self-assessment should serve as a challenge to every one of us to take a serious look in the metaphorical mirror.

Are my microbehaviors landing in a constructive way? Do they advance the business agenda? Do they advance the development and success of others? Do they create a culture of engagement and inclusivity? These are the kinds of questions we should be asking ourselves as we set this book down.

While this book is clearly aimed at people with managerial responsibilities, I can't help but point out that pretty much everything covered in the book applies to everyone in a workplace, not just managers. Imagine a jobsite where everyone's microbehaviors are positive, constructive, and productive. Wouldn't that be an engaging and perhaps even self-actualized place to spend your days?

My advice? After assessing and taking actions to improve your microbehaviors, pass along a copy of this book to someone you believe could benefit from its insights. And don't just pass it along but ask that person to read it and then discuss it with you. Then ask him or her to do the same with another person. Pay it forward.

No, wait. Instead of passing it along to one person for a discussion, how about passing it along to two people for a discussion and then asking them to pass it along to two others? That way, the word about microbehaviors grows exponentially rather than arithmetically, like a virtuous pyramid scheme. It can be your personal contribution to making the world a better place to work.

—Steve King
Author of *Brag, Worry, Wonder, Bet: A Manager's Guide to Giving Feedback* (2013); *Six Conversations: A Simple Guide for Managerial Success* (2015); *Alignment, Process, Relationships: A Simple Guide to Team Management* (2019); and *The Manager's Dilemma: A Manager's Guide to Change Management* (2022)

ADDITIONAL READING

Here are a few excellent books you'll enjoy. I love the practical advice in them. I've mentioned most of them already throughout this book.

Allen, James B. *As a Man Thinketh.* New York: Simon & Schuster, 1903

Carnegie, Dale. *How to Win Friends and Influence People.* New York: Simon & Schuster, 1998.

Covey, Steven R. *The 7 Habits of Highly Effective People: 30th Anniversary Edition.* New York: Simon & Schuster, 2020.

Goleman, Daniel. *Emotional Intelligence: Why It Can Matter More Than IQ. 25th Anniversary Edition.* London: Bloomsbury Publishing, 2020.

King, Steve. *Alignment, Process, Relationships: A Simple Guide to Team Management.* Bloomington, IN: iUniverse, 2019.

———. *Brag, Worry, Wonder, Bet: A Manager's Guide to Giving Feedback.* Bloomington, IN: iUniverse, 2013.

———. *The Manager's Dilemma: A Manager's Guide to Change Management*. Bloomington, IN: iUniverse, 2022.

———. *Six Conversations: A Simple Guide for Managerial Success*. Bloomington, IN: iUniverse, 2015.

Peale, Norman Vincent. *The Power of Positive Thinking*. New York: Simon & Schuster, 2015.

Singh, Deanna. *Actions Speak Louder: A Step-by-Step Guide to Becoming an Inclusive Workplace*. New York: Penguin Random House, 2022.

Winters, Mary-Frances. *Black Fatigue*. Oakland, CA: Berrett-Koehler Publishers, 2020.

———. *Inclusive Conversations*. Oakland, CA: Berrett-Koehler Publishers, 2020.

———. *We Can't Talk about That at Work*. Oakland, CA: Berrett-Koehler Publishers, 2017.

Printed in the United States
by Baker & Taylor Publisher Services